TWICKENHAM
MOTORCARS

A LOCAL HISTOR
MANUFAC1

ROBIN HUNTER

Paper Number 108

Price £10.50

First published 2024

The Borough of Twickenham Local History Society
http://botlhs.co.uk/

© Robin Hunter, 2024

British Library Cataloguing in Publication Data.
A catalogue record for this book is available from the British Library.

ISBN 978-1-911145-08-0

Printed in Great Britain

Dedication.

To the Eel Pie Island Museum,
where my journey began
and to my great-grandfather
Henry Cornelius Hunter,
about whom I discovered
so much more during my research.

CONTENTS

Preface   7

1. **Introduction**   9

2. **Why Twickenham?**   14

3. **The Orleans Cars and Orleans Motor Works**   18
    Burford, van Toll and the New Orleans Motor Company   18
    Orleans Motor Company   24
    Orleans Motor Works   31

4. **Johannes van Toll: Twickenham's motoring pioneer**   38

5. **Not just cars … buses too.**   45
    Beaufort Motor Company   45
    Scott, Stirling & Co. Ltd.   47

6. **Twickenham vehicles before and just after World War 1**   51
    Corben's Carriage factory and Twickenham Motor Co.   51
    Wyvern Light Cars   55
    Palladium Autocars and Autovan   56
    Mercury Cars Ltd.   58
    Taunton Cars Ltd.   61
    The Lington Engineering Co. Ltd.   62
    Straker-Squire Ltd.   65
    Berliet Motor and Engineering Co. Ltd.   68

7. **Twickenham's motorbikes**   71
    Grigg Motorcycles   71
    Martinshaw Motorcycles   73
    Wooler Engineering Co.   74
    WGC Hayward & Co.   75
    Argson Engineering Co.   76
    Packman & Poppe Ltd.   77
    F M Avey of Teddington   78

8. **Vehicles made in Teddington, Hampton Hill and Hampton**   79
    The Carden Monocar and Ward & Avey Ltd.   79
    Teddington Motorcar and Launch Works   84
    Monarch Motor Co. Ltd.   84
    British Anzani Engineering Co.   86
    AC Cars at Tagg's Island, Hampton   90

9. Local motoring family businesses   94

Tamplin's of Twickenham   94
Kingsbury's of Hampton   99
CA Blay at Twickenham Green   100
Palmer's of Teddington   102
Mercury Motors, Twickenham   105
Elijah Thornton and Arlington Works   110
P & S Motors Ltd, and Palmer Coachbuilder Ltd, Teddington   112

10. A Motoring Renaissance: Twickenham's racing cars   114

Emeryson Cars Ltd.   114
Bob Spikins, his cars and Spikins Garage   118
John Willment Automobiles   121
Bracey-Price and David Price Racing   125
Racing Services Partnership   127
The Costin-Nathan car   128

Appx I.   **Henry Cornelius Hunter, my great grandfather**   132

Appx II.   **Twickenham motor racing driver, Roberta Cowell**   140

Appx III.   **New Orleans cars still in existence**   142

Appx IV.   **New Orleans Voiturette Handbook and Specifications 1900**   153

Appx V.   **The Orleans Motor Co. Ltd. Catalogue c1907**   156

Appx VI.   **Plans: Orleans Motor Works 1903 and 1914**   167

List of figures: maps, photographs and illustrations   170

References   185

Acknowledgements   188

PREFACE

I HAD NO IDEA what a journey of discovery I was embarking upon when I first started to research Twickenham's motorcars. Having been a keen motoring enthusiast all my life, I was intrigued to read that Frederick Simms, the *'father of the British motor industry'* [1], had a strong Twickenham connection. I discovered this at the Eel Pie Island Museum as a volunteer, soon after it opened in 2018. I had no idea that Twickenham, the town where I grew up, had any motoring heritage at all. It was also a surprise to learn that Eel Pie Island, where I lived as a child, had played a key role in the fledgling British motor industry. Even more amazing, was to uncover a direct family link to the boatyards on the Eel Pie Island and to the Orleans Motor Company, Twickenham's first car maker. This book also covers the more modest motor industry in other parts of the old Borough of Twickenham.

I have contacted every museum and motor vehicle collection that I could find listed, in my search for surviving Twickenham cars. If any reader knows of any other surviving vehicles, other Twickenham cars or has any

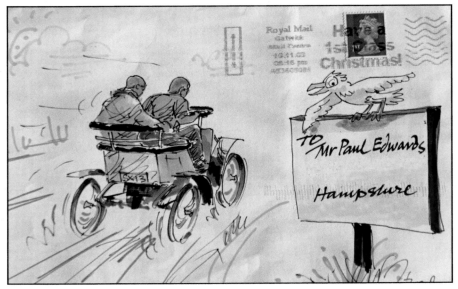

Fig 1

stories or information about them, I would love to hear from you. Please make contact via botlhs@gmail.com.

The Twickenham built motor vehicles shown on the cover of this book are: a 1919 Mercury; a 1951 Emeryson Formula 3 racing car; a 1900 New Orleans Voiturette; a 1956 Willment-Climax sports-racer; a 1950s British Anzani Astra Utility; a 1928 Berliet tipper-truck and a 1920s Packman and Poppe two-stroke motorcycle.

The author is at the wheel of SX 13 in the photograph on the back of this book.

The cartoon *(fig 1)* was drawn on an envelope addressed to Paul Edwards, owner of New Orleans Voiturette SX 13, almost certainly Twickenham's oldest surviving car.

1. INTRODUCTION

IT IS WIDELY accepted that the British motor industry started in Coventry in 1897 with the first British Daimler car. However, British involvement in the internal combustion engine had already been established by Frederick Simms on the banks of the River Thames between Fulham and Twickenham, well before Britain's first motorcar factory was opened. Motorboats had been in production since the early 1890s, before cars were allowed to use Britain's roads freely. Motorboats, first electric powered, then petrol driven, had been in production on Eel Pie Island in Twickenham since 1893.

The first production car on Britain's roads was imported into Britain from France by Evelyn Henry Ellis in June 1895. Before this, there had been a handful of British cars, essentially one-off inventions. Probably the earliest is Edward Butler's *'Petrol Cycle'* in 1888. The Petrol Cycle had three bicycle-style wheels and a petrol engine under the seat. This was earlier than the car designed by Karl Benz, generally recognised to be the world's first motorcar. By 1892, William Bremer had built the first all-British petrol-engined four-wheeler motorcar. Although he built a second car with a four-cylinder engine, it didn't go into production. His original car has survived and can be seen at the Vestry House Museum in Walthamstow, where Bremer built the car. Others followed, like the Santler brothers in Malvern with their *'Dogcart'*. They are also credited with giving Evelyn Ellis (mentioned earlier) his first driving lesson. The *'1894 Santler Dogcart, believed to be Britain's oldest car'* was auctioned by Bonhams in 2017.

Also in 1894, George William Lanchester built the first all-British motorboat. Although this was a year or two after the Daimler motorboats built on the Thames, Frederick Simms was of course using German Daimler engines. Interestingly, James Dennis Roots was using oil to power a ferry between Richmond and Wandsworth in 1891 and 1892, along the same stretch of the Thames and at the same time that Johannes van Toll was trialling the Daimler petrol engine. The two vessels would doubtless have passed each other. Roots then produced a two-stroke

Fig 2

tricycle which ran on heavy oil in 1892. Rudolph Diesel designed and built his first Diesel engine using heavy oil as a fuel in Germany in 1893/4. Roots' three-wheeler motorcar was almost certainly the first British heavy-oil (diesel) car and a year before Diesel's engine.

By the end of 1895, fourteen or fifteen cars are believed to have been on Britain's roads. The photograph *(fig 2)*, taken at a parade in Eastbourne c1897, shows Simms' Daimler heralding the death knell of the horse drawn age of road transport in Britain. At that time there were already several bicycle makers established in Twickenham. One would go on to produce Twickenham's first motorcar. There were also a number of carriage builders who would quickly adapt to building the coachwork for motor vehicles. The third and most important ingredient for Twickenham's early involvement with motorcar manufacture was the pioneering motor engineering that took place on Eel Pie Island. The building of motorboats by Frederick Simms' Daimler Motor company, which preceded motorcar building in Britain, had created a trained local workforce of motor engineers.

In 1900 the first Twickenham built car, the New Orleans Voiturette, went on sale. By then, the number of cars on Britain's roads had reached seven or eight hundred. By 1904, numbers had reached 23,000. In 1910, the

100,000 mark was passed. That number had exceeded a million by the beginning of the 1930s and by the 2020s there were more than 38 million cars on Britain's roads.

By the outbreak of the First World War, the Mercury, Wyvern and other Twickenham motorcars were in production. The borough was becoming a significant motor manufacturing centre. As the map *(fig 3, overleaf)* shows, local motor producers established themselves within a few hundred yards of Eel Pie Island, where Twickenham's motoring story began. If one business failed, another would take over, often in the same factory, probably using the same machinery and undoubtedly the same workforce of skilled engineers.

During the First World War, engineering output was switched to the war effort. By then, manufacturing for aircraft production had started in Twickenham, with the Sopwith Aviation company already established at nearby Kingston in 1912. After the war, the factories and works returned to motor manufacturing and were about to enjoy the heyday of local motor manufacturing. Interestingly most of the vehicles were aimed at aspiring motorists from the lower-middle or working classes. Many were troops returning from war, keen to become motorists having taken part in a bloody and motorised war.

By the 1920s, factories were producing a range of motor vehicles including motorbikes like the Grigg, motor scooters like the Whippet, trucks, charabancs and, earlier, buses. Unfortunately, this heyday for Twickenham's motor industry was to be short lived. The postwar boom turned to bust, a result of the global economic depression, an inability to react quickly enough to changes in the market, and changes in production methods.

Large volume car and motorcycle manufacturers were now dominating the market, using production-line methods and benefitting from the economies of mass production. The motor works in Twickenham, producing small numbers of hand-built motor vehicles, could not compete. Virtually all motor manufacturing in the Twickenham area had ceased by 1926.

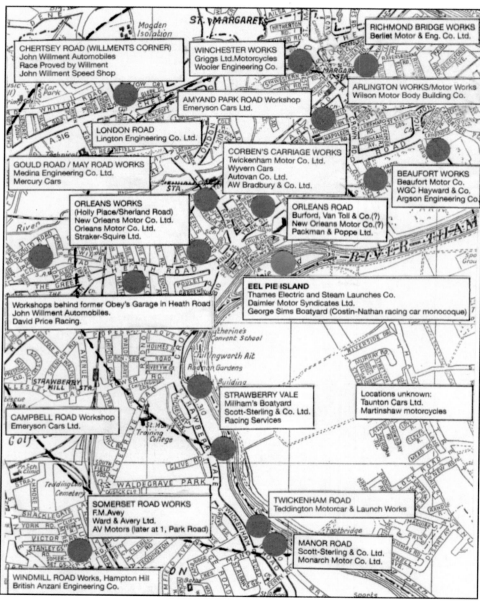

CHERTSEY ROAD (WILLMENTS CORNER)
John Willment Automobiles
Race Proved by Willment
John Willment Speed Shop

WINCHESTER WORKS
Griggs Ltd.Motorcycles
Wooler Engineering Co.

RICHMOND BRIDGE WORKS
Berliet Motor & Eng. Co. Ltd.

AMYAND PARK ROAD Workshop
Emeryson Cars Ltd.

ARLINGTON WORKS/Motor Works
Wilson Motor Body Building Co.

LONDON ROAD
Lington Engineering Co. Ltd.

CORBEN'S CARRIAGE WORKS
Twickenham Motor Co. Ltd.
Wyvern Cars
Autovan Co. Ltd.
AW Bradbury & Co. Ltd.

GOULD ROAD / MAY ROAD WORKS
Medina Engineering Co. Ltd.
Mercury Cars

BEAUFORT WORKS
Beaufort Motor Co.
WGC Hayward & Co.
Argson Engineering Co.

ORLEANS WORKS
(Holly Place/Sherland Road)
New Orleans Motor Co. Ltd.
Orleans Motor Co. Ltd.
Straker-Squire Ltd.

ORLEANS ROAD
Burford, Van Toll & Co.(?)
New Orleans Motor Co.(?)
Packman & Poppe Ltd.

EEL PIE ISLAND
Thames Electric and Steam Launches Co.
Daimler Motor Syndicates Ltd.
George Sims Boatyard (Costin-Nathan racing car monocoque)

Workshops behind former Obey's Garage in Heath Road
John Willment Automobiles.
David Price Racing.

STRAWBERRY VALE
Millham's Boatyard
Scott-Sterling & Co. Ltd.
Racing Services

Locations unknown:
Taunton Cars Ltd.
Martinshaw motorcycles

CAMPBELL ROAD Workshop
Emeryson Cars Ltd.

SOMERSET ROAD WORKS
F.M.Avey
Ward & Avery Ltd.
AV Motors (later at 1, Park Road)

TWICKENHAM ROAD
Teddington Motorcar & Launch Works

MANOR ROAD
Scott-Sterling & Co. Ltd.
Monarch Motor Co. Ltd.

WINDMILL ROAD Works, Hampton Hill
British Anzani Engineering Co.

Fig 3

Twickenham's engineering motor works together with the skilled labour force then turned to making motorcar parts and commercial vehicle bodies instead. However, motor works situated on the river did continue to make motorboats.

There was a small scale but important renaissance in specialist motor engineering in Twickenham in the second half of 20th century, including a number of successful racing car makers.

Despite this, the industry is now all but forgotten. This book seeks to put Twickenham back on the motoring road map.

2. WHY TWICKENHAM?

O F COURSE, TWICKENHAM was not the only place where early developments in British motor transport were taking place during the 1880s and 1890s. Engineers and inventors in many parts of the country were working independently in small workshops to this end. Some of the testing had to be done on water as the Locomotives Act virtually prohibited motor transport on Britain's roads. Others risked breaking the law.

Many pioneers were essentially inventors, whose prototypes never went into production. Many also claimed to have invented the first British motorcar, like George Lanchester and William Bremer mentioned earlier, also Harry Lawson, who was later to take control of Daimler from Simms. There is no evidence for Lawson's claim but he was responsible for '*the first authentic design of safety bicycle employing chain-drive to the rear wheel*' [2]. Lawson is credited, with John Kemp Stanley, for inventing the modern bicycle.

Once the '*Red Flag Act*' was repealed, the British motor industry had to play catch up with other countries, principally Germany, France and America to get Britain's roads motorised.

Twickenham's importance as a motor manufacturing centre is confirmed by the list of '*Automobile Manufacturers and Assemblers in the UK up to 1914*' compiled by *Grace's Guide to British Industrial History*. The list has around 550 entries. Interestingly, almost half of those listed survived for less than two years.

Most large industrial cities in Britain can claim at least a handful of motor manufacturers. However Birmingham and Coventry, where Britain's first motorcar factory was established, each have over 30 marques listed. London can claim well over 100, with motor manufacturers spread fairly evenly across the capital. Kensington stands out as a particular centre with six entries, followed by Willesden with five.

There are groupings of makers in the suburbs south and west of London. Here Twickenham stands out, with the six motor manufacturers to be identified in Chapters 3 and 6, plus one in Teddington (Chapter 8) and two bus

Fig 4

makers (Chapter 5) [3]. Twickenham borough has a total of nine. Twickenham's immediate neighbours, Richmond and Kingston, each have two and Thames Ditton and nearby Weybridge have three each. Although perhaps not a definitive list of motor manufacturers in Britain, this list does nevertheless add weight to the claim that Twickenham was amongst the earliest British motor manufacturing centres.

The reason this happened in Twickenham goes back to 1889 when, whilst working in Germany, Frederick Simms became friends with Gottlieb Daimler. He bought the rights to produce Daimler's petrol engine in Britain and sent the Dutch engineer, Johannes van Toll, to London in May 1890. His task was to test and trial the engine on the River Thames. Simms demonstrated a Daimler engined motor launch to the public on the Thames in 1891. The motoring pioneer Evelyn Ellis ordered the first of several Simms' motor launches in the same year. In 1893 Simms established Daimler Motor Syndicates, widely recognised as Britain's first motor company. Also in 1893 Simms was introduced to Andrew Pears who owned the hotel and boatyard on Eel Pie Island.

Daimler Motor Syndicates was first established under a railway arch at Putney Bridge Station in Fulham to import, build and use German Daimler petrol engines,. They soon moved to the boatyard on Eel Pie Island, seen in the photograph *(fig 4)*. Here, innovative electric-powered launches were already being built by William Sargeant. The contract for

15

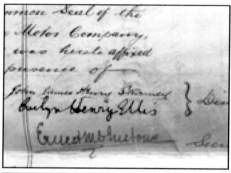

Frederick Simms to buy the Eel Pie Island boatyard from Andrew Pears and the Pears Soap family is witnessed by Evelyn Ellis, *(figs 5a/b/c)*. *Fig 5c* shows the seal of Daimler Motor Company Ltd.

Simms' Daimler launches were almost certainly the first serial-production petrol-engined transport to be built in Britain and played a key role in establishing Britain's motor industry. The work done on the River Thames between Putney Bridge and Eel Pie Island in Twickenham was laying the foundations for the British motor industry.

By the mid 1890s, Frederick Simms was making plans to build motorcars, not in Twickenham but near Cheltenham. This was to be the first purpose-built motorcar factory in Britain. In the end, a converted mill in Coventry was chosen as Daimler Motors' factory and the first British built Daimler

Figs 5a, 5b and 5c

motorcar went on sale to the public in January 1897. At about this time Simms also started building motorboats at Daimler's new Coventry manufacturing base. Daimler's operations on Eel Pie Island were coming to an end.

Johannes van Toll, Simms' chief engineer on Eel Pie Island, appears however to have continued building launches on the island whilst also setting up a motorcar manufacturing company in Twickenham with another former Daimler employee, Henry Burford. For van Toll, building motorcars was an obvious development from building motorboats. Since 1896, Henry Burford had been involved in bicycle making at The Orleans Cycle Works in King Street, Twickenham.

Fig 6

When Burford and van Toll set up in business to make and sell motorcars, they were already two years behind the front runners like Daimler. Their plan, therefore, was to select a car already tried and tested that could be launched on to the market straight away. They found a suitable candidate: a Belgian car that was already proven and that had been praised in the British motoring press. The first model sold by van Toll and Burford was the Vivinus Voiturette (small car) which had been launched in Belgium in July 1899. Their advertising slogan read, *'the simplest and best two-seated car made'*, seen in the advertisement *(fig 6)*.

Twickenham's first production car could be described as a European venture. The Voiturette went into production in Belgium, Germany, France and Britain. Frederick Simms was German born, although his grandfather was from Birmingham. He has been described as *'the catalyst and intermediary between Britain and Europe'*. [4] Johannes van Toll, who set up the New Orleans company with Henry Burford, was Dutch. Burford was British, born in Matlock, Derbyshire. The Voiturette was a Belgian design from Ateliers Vivinus who were based near Brussels. However, Alexis Vivinus who developed the car was born in Senay in the Jura region of France.

It was to be a highly successful and truly European enterprise.

3. THE ORLEANS CARS AND ORLEANS MOTOR WORKS

IN 1899 JOHANNES van Toll teamed up with Henry Burford, a former Daimler colleague and Frederick Arnold Rodewald to build cars in Twickenham. They formed Burford, Van Toll and Company. The Thames Valley Motor Company was then created on 14th September 1899 to manufacture their first car, the New Orleans. Burford, Van Toll and Co. was dissolved and in 1901, the New Orleans Motor Company was formed.

But why did Burford and van Toll name their car the New Orleans? Henry Burford was already making the Orleans cycle. The Orleans name was taken from Twickenham's connections with the Duc d'Orleans in the early 19th century. Why the car was called the *New* Orleans rather than the Orleans is unclear. However, this could have been to avoid confusion with a company owned by E. H. Owen, of West Kensington, called the Orlean Car Co. Charles Rolls apparently suggested they drop the New from the name. [5] They changed the name of the company to the Orleans Motor Company in 1905. At least in part this was to dispel any suggestion that the company might be American, instead suggesting that it was French!

Burford, van Toll and the New Orleans Motor Company

Burford and van Toll visited Brussels in 1899 to view the Vivinus Voiturette, which had been selected as the car that they would build under license in Twickenham. Van Toll and Burford met Alexis Vivinus to inspect and test his little car. Born in 1860, Vivinus had also built the first Belgium motorcycle in 1896. He started work on the Voiturette in 1898 and launched the model in July 1899. Burford and van Toll *'concluded that in every respect this car fills the requirement'* according to Autocar magazine in February 1900. Van Toll was reported to have driven the car from Brussels to Namur and back again, returning in low gear to test the engine's cooling system. The first New Orleans cars were imported directly or assembled from parts imported from Belgium but with modifications and, of course, the New Orleans badge on the front, as seen in the photograph *(fig 7)*. The company soon started to produce and source parts locally so that the cars were nearer to their own model. The Voiturette was described at the time in Autocar magazine as *'a smart racy looking little car'*. It had two seats and a vertical steering column, as the photograph of Johannes van Toll driving the Voiturette shows *(fig 8)*.

Fig 7

The New Orleans Voiturette was a success … small, basic, cheap and reliable. It went on sale at the dawn of British motoring and, and as Autocar in 1900 suggests, out to capture a new market. The New Orleans Voiturette was *'to satisfy the autocar cravings of the class once described by Carlisle as the gigmanity, those who do not care to or cannot afford to pay anything from £250 to £600 for a car'*, but if… *'a little vehicle to carry two or three at a pinch, could be obtained for something under £150, would shortly be found driving their own cars about the country in hundreds '*[6]. A somewhat patronising tone but a view that proved prophetic as it was this market that most Twickenham cars set out to satisfy. Edward Tamplin described the Voiturette as *'a real "light" car'* [7]. The mould had been set for the Twickenham Light car.

Burford and van Toll advertised widely, promoting their little car's advantages over

Fig 8

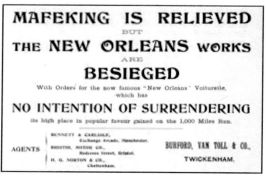

Fig 9

Fig 10

its competitors, as the advertisement from 1900 shows *(fig 9)*. They were also happy to exploit current events, like the relief of Mafeking during the Boer War, to promote their cars. The seven-month siege of Mafeking in South Africa came to an end on 17th May 1900. This advertisement also shows that they were developing a network of agents around the country.

Two New Orleans cars competed in an *'Across Britain 1000-Mile Trial'*, which proved a valuable testing ground and resulted in many orders. This success was, of course, used in their advertising *(fig 10)*.

Six hundred New Orleans cars were sold in the first two years of production, many more than the original Vivinus in Belgium. All the New Orleans cars assembled in Twickenham were built under license from Vivinus. Burford and van Toll had secured the patents for the car in Britain and America. The link with Vivinus was strengthened in 1901 when the New Orleans Motor Co Ltd. was formed with directors from both companies.

The first Voiturettes had a 3.5 horsepower, air cooled, single-cylinder engine, mounted transversely. The body was a very light (3.5 cwt) two-seater, open to the elements. The original Belgian car had a two-speed gearbox, but the British model was fitted with three speeds and better brakes. In *Autocar* magazine of September 1900 the company was praised for introducing an ingenious new float carburettor. The cars were very competitively priced at £140, cheaper than most rivals, and were advertised for their strength and reliability.

The New Orleans Vivinus-based models remained in production with various modifications until at least 1905. The company had already added a twin-cylinder 6 hp car to their range by October 1900, followed by a 7 hp also using a Vivinus design. The first two-cylinder engines were basically two engines working side by side, sharing the same carburettor. The photograph *(fig 11a)* shows the engine of the sole surviving twin-cylinder Voiturette, 8710 MN (formerly AX 74) and the air-cooled transverse engine made from two single-cylinder engines joined by the flywheel.

Fig 11b

The photograph *(fig 11b)* shows the driver's basic controls on a 1900 Voiturette. Note that the clutch and footbrake are on the opposite sides to modern cars, and the throttle (accelerator) is on the steering column not on the floor. The present pattern of foot pedals only became established in the 1920s with the Austin 7.

Ching & Co. produced a series of 50 cigarette cards entitled '*Veteran and Vintage Cars*' in 1960. Card No.4 was the New Orleans (1900), as seen in the photographs *(figs 12a/b)*.

On 8th February 1902, two New Orleans cars took part in a series of hill tests up Richmond Hill from the Dysart Arms to the Star and Garter Hotel, a distance of 600 yards. One Voiturette achieved almost 16 mph

Figs 12a and 12b

up the steep slope despite poor weather and thick mud. With just 12 hp, it came third, behind a 16 hp Napier, and a 20 hp Milne driven by Henry Burford. This was not the first time that the hill had been used to test the hill climbing abilities of motorcars. As part of the 1899 *Automobile Club Show* in Richmond (advertised in the poster *(fig 13)*) cars competed up the same stretch of hill. The photograph of this very early event shows a Lanchester in action *(fig 14)*.

In the afternoon of the 1902 event, they moved on to Test Hill between Robin Hood and Kingston Gates in Richmond Park. This was a longer and steeper hill climb with a bend. The New Orleans car also maintained its podium position in this contest. New Orleans Voiturettes won numerous medals at trials in Britain and abroad.

Fig 13

By early 1902 work was underway on a new 14 hp four-cylinder car with a four-speed gearbox. At about the same time, Vivinus in Belgium launched a similar 14 hp car. This would suggest collaboration between the two companies as a result of them sharing directors after 1901. Vivinus also launched a 9 hp water-cooled twin cylinder model. By 1903, this model was offered by New Orleans and priced at £294. By the end of 1903, the 14 hp car had been phased out and replaced by two new four-cylinder models, a 12 hp at £398 and a 15 hp at £561. A 1904 15 hp model can be seen in the photograph *(fig 15)*.

Fig 14

As well as being produced in Belgium and Britain, the Voiturette was built under license by De Dietrich in Germany and Georges Richard in France. The Richard model, called the Pony, was longer and was better appointed than the original Belgian or early British cars. It had the addition of two rear seats or a large wicker boot behind the front seats and a raked steering column, much improving the driving position. A very handsome Richard Pony has participated in the London to Brighton Run in recent years. The photograph *(fig 16)* shows Tim Summers' 1901 3.5 hp single-

Fig 15

Fig 16

cylinder model, BS 8654, at Brighton having completed the run in November 2019. A number of New Orleans Voiturettes join up to 500 cars in the annual London to Brighton Veteran Car Run (see Appendix III).

The New Orleans Voiturette had been an undoubted success but by 1905 it was dated. Rapid developments had been taking place in motor engineering and motorcar design. An ambitious programme of new models was launched under the new name, the Orleans Motor Company.

Orleans Motor Company

From 1905 the Orleans company concentrated on larger cars with four and six-cylinder engines. By then, all production was taking place in the purpose-built motor works in Holly Place between Holly Road and Sherland Road in Twickenham. The extent of the new factory can be seen in the Goad Fire Insurance map of 1907 *(fig 17, opposite page)*. The site is marked *'Orleans Motor Co. Ltd.'* towards the top right of the map. The aerial photograph of central Twickenham looking north, shows the Cross Deep junction with King Street before it was widened. In the foreground (bottom right), No.12 King Street is clearly visible on the corner. The Orleans Works, built between Sherland Road and Holly Place, can be seen towards the top left of the photograph *(fig 18)*.

Fig 18

24

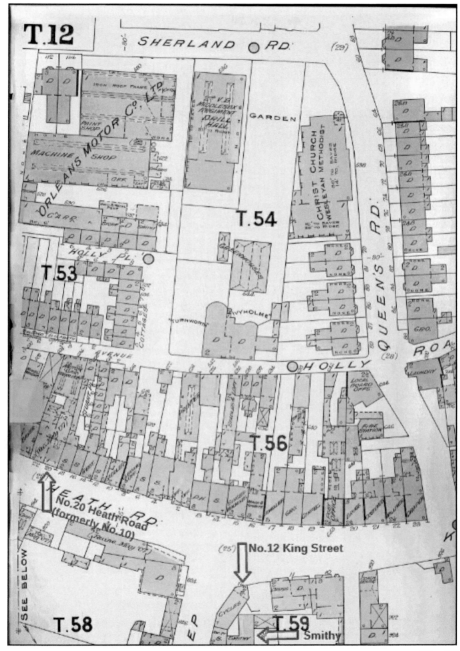

Fig 17

25

Four-cylinder 22 and 25 hp (3498 and 4560 cc) engined cars had appeared by 1905 and a six-cylinder 30/35 hp (6840 cc) car in 1906. Orleans boasted that their cars were *'now all British made'*.[7] By the middle of the first decade of the 1900s there was a thriving motorcar components industry in Britain, not least in Twickenham. This was able to supply all the parts necessary to build the Orleans cars. The bodywork may have been built at the factory; the map of the site (Appendix VI) does show a paint shop though this was probably for painting the cars' chassis. It seems more likely, however, that the car bodies were built by one of a number of specialist coach builders only a few hundred yards away. By 1907, the new works was already being outgrown. An article in *The Morning Post* on 26th January 1907 suggests *'space at Twickenham is limited and the business has outgrown the capacity of the 100 hands or so that are employed'*.

The Manager of the Orleans works was William Henry Astell, who lived at 67, Queens Road between 1901 and 1910. He also provided numerous technical innovations in the development of the Orleans cars. Astell was a works driver in motoring competitions and represented the company on many occasions. He had joined the New Orleans Motor Co. in its earliest

Fig 19

days and *'drove a New Orleans car successfully through the 1000 miles Trial in 1900'* [8]. Astell may previously have worked on Eel Pie Island, as he had *'connections with automobilism at an early date, having owned and driven a motor boat fitted with a petrol motor in 1894, and a 4 h.p. Panhard car in 1896'*. Astell was also described as a *'motor car maker, working on own account'* [8] though there is no evidence that he actually built his own cars.

The Orleans Company built on the performance trials successes of the New Orleans cars. Orleans cars achieved 7th and 9th places in the 1905 International Tourist Trophy held by the Royal

Automobile Club on the Isle of Man, trailing not far behind the likes of John Napier, and Charles Rolls who was driving an early Rolls-Royce. The Orleans cars averaged 28 mph and 29 mph over the gruelling 208 mile course, whilst Napier and Rolls managed a slightly quicker 32 mph. Many of the other entries did not even complete the lengthy course. The

Fig 20

1905 Certificate of Performance *(shown in fig 19)* was awarded for the 15 hp Orleans car at the Tourist Trophy Race on the Isle of Man held on 14th September 1905.. The driver, Thomas Jenner, was another local motoring pioneer. By 1901 he was already a trained motor

Fig 21

engineer although only 18 years old. A copy of the Certificate of Performance was hanging on the office wall of Orleans Motors, Richmond Road in 2018 (see Chapter 4). The 1905 advertisement *(fig 20)* for the 15 hp Orleans car boasts *'fastest car at the price'*.

The photograph *(fig 21)* shows a 15 hp model of the period. Another photograph *(fig 22)* shows what was described in the manufacturer's brochure as the *'Four-Cylinder Chassis, with tyres'* and the 30-40 hp engine. Rolls & Co were appointed as the London agents for these new, large and well-appointed Orleans' cars and a showroom was rented at Carlton House in Regent Street. Orleans cars gained some loyal and prestigious customers: Earl Cairns, a prominent Conservative states-man and Lord Chancellor, owned a 7 hp twin in 1902, progressed to a 15 hp

Fig 22

four-cylinder in 1905 and then on to a 35 hp six-cylinder model with a detachable top in May 1907.

The Amir of Afghanistan used a 22 hp Orleans car to make a tour of India in 1908; it was the first motorcar he had travelled in. *'The Ameer expressed such delight in its smooth running and range of speed that the Indian Government purchased a 22hp Orleans and presented it to his majesty'* (King Edward VII).[9]. One Orleans car took Major Godfrey, a political agent and his wife from Nowshera to Dargai through the Malakand Pass. As well as driving through a river, axle deep, it ascended 3000 feet with a continuous climb of six miles. They returned via the Swat Valley *'without accident or trouble to the car'*.[9] It was reported that Orleans cars became particularly successful in India.

Another loyal - and local - customer was Dr Langdon Down, who established Normansfield Hospital in Teddington to treat those with developmental and intellectual impairment. He gave his name to the condition Down's Syndrome. Langdon Down owned a 1905 35 hp limousine *(fig 23)*, a 1906 22 hp Landaulet, and a very handsome 1907 35hp open tourer, like the one shown in the advertisement *(fig 24)*, described in *Autocar* as *'sold at a moderate price as six-cylinder vehicles go, at £975'*. It was also praised for *'its technical detail and the carriage-work... excellently finished throughout and in every way a credit to British workmanship!'* [10]. This car, FX 344, exhibited by Orleans Cars at the 1907 Olympia Motor Show, illustrates the progress the company had made in car design in just a few years. This car could be said to have

Fig 23

more in common with a modern car than with the Voiturette.

1907 MODEL

35-H.P. 6-Cylinder Orleans Car

PRICE, complete, with Side Entrance Body, upholstered in Leather, painted in any colour,

£975

Fig 24

At least one other engineering company was engaged to produce Orleans Motor Co. models. *The Evening Star* reported on 7th September 1906 that E.& F. Turner of Ipswich had started a co-operative venture with Orleans cars. They would assemble the Orleans six-cylinder 35 hp model at their St. Peter's Ironworks factory and, once assembled and tested, the cars would be sent to Twickenham to have *'roomy and comfortable' bodies fitted.'* The article also reported that the driver or *'chauffeur... could regulate the speed... by the use of the foot-speed accelerator'*. Orleans cars clearly now used an accelerator foot pedal rather than a hand operated throttle. Turner manufactured one car a week with plans to produce more.

However, the competition was becoming stiffer with an increasing number of motor manufacturers, and while most early cars had been hand-made locally and in small numbers, this was about to change. Relatively few of the up-market Orleans models were made. In 1910, only two models remained in production. No Orleans cars at all were exhibited at any of the 1910 motor shows. Soon after, Orleans disappeared from the market altogether. The company closed and went into liquidation at the end of the same year.

The closure of the company had been coming for a little while. There was a report in the press of legal proceedings against the company at Marlborough Street Magistrates' Court in 1909. The Orleans Motor Company had not been paying the agreed rent of £1250 per annum for the Regent Street office and showroom since early in 1908, a period of *'a year and nine months'*. Mr Lorden, the landlord, had only been paid £400 on account, so took possession of three cars (interestingly, *not* Orleans cars) kept at the premises, in lieu of the unpaid rent, which amounted to £1037.10 shillings. It was reported that Lorden had been keeping an eye on the premises in order to *'see how well the cars sold, with a view to his rent'*. He had understood that all the cars were owned by the company, so felt justified in seizing them. However, Frederick Rodewell, a director of the Orleans company since it was formed in 1905, claimed that he had proof of buying the cars himself, so they were his own private property and not the property of the company. Nevertheless, Mr.Denman, the magistrate reached the conclusion that it had been reasonable for Mr Lorden to take the cars *'as security'* for unpaid rent, as reported in *The Gazette*, Saturday 25th December 1909. This proved to be a rather inauspicious prelude to the liquidation and dissolution of the company the following year and a sad end to the first of Twickenham's motorcar manufacturers.

After the success of the small, light and cheap New Orleans cars and failure of the larger, more luxurious Orleans cars, Twickenham motor manufacturers returned to making cheaper lighter vehicles again and went on to become a centre for light car manufacture.

Unlike New Orleans cars, no Orleans cars appear to have survived.

Large volume car manufacturers were now starting to dominate the market. By 1907, Henry Ford's cars were starting to be imported from America through their UK concessionaire, Perry, Thornton & Schreiber Ltd. The cover of their 1907 brochure is shown below *(fig 25)*. They were offering the Model N for only £165. They were already using

mass-production methods, as the photograph from the brochure *(fig 26)* of the Model N under construction shows. This factory alone was producing 45 cars a day, six days a week, totalling over 10,000 new Model Ns a year. By 1908 the Model N was being imported into Britain, manufactured using assembly-line techniques for the first time. In 1909, the year

Fig 25

Fig 26

before Orleans cars disappeared from the market, Ford became established in Britain.

Orleans Motor Works

The original Orleans Works was commonly thought to have been at the corner of Orleans and Chapel Road in Twickenham. The map shows the location of the Orleans Road site, marked *'Works' (fig 27)*. This has long been referred to by local historians and motoring writers alike. There is a reference to *'Burford and Van Toll of Orleans Road, Twickenham'* in the seminal *History of Motoring and Motorcars* written by the technical editor of *The Motor,* which was published in 1956 and so within living memory of the Orleans company.

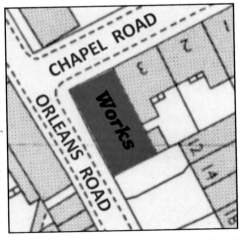

Fig 27

Fig 28

However, recent research has placed the company's first location in central Twickenham. The premises at No.12 King Street, believed to have been owned by William Tamplin, had been rented to H.G.Burford & Co. as *'The Orleans Cycle Works'* between 1896 and 1900. It can be seen at the far right of the 1896 photograph *(fig 28)* of King Street on the day that the circus came to town. The location is shown between Wharf Lane and Cross Deep on the 1907 Goad map of King Street *(see fig 17)*.

One of the earliest references to the Voiturette, in *The Motor-Car Journal* on 19th January 1900, interestingly referred to it *'being constructed and put on the market by... the Orleans Cycle and Motor Works, Twickenham'* [11].

Letters have recently come to light in a collection of materials about New Orleans Voiturette AX 74, when it was owned by Sir Clive Edwards (see Appendix III). Sir Clive bought the car in 1944 from the original owner and set about trying to find out more about the Voiturette. He wrote to the Tamplin family and received a reply from Edward Tamplin, motor engineer (see Chapter 9), son of William Tamplin mentioned above. In his reply, Tamplin states that the Voiturette *'... was first made when I was a boy... at 12 King Street'.* He later refers to *'when the car works moved to ... Orleans Road'*[(12)]. However, his letters contain a number of inconsistencies and cannot be totally relied upon. The premises on the corner of Orleans Road and Chapel Road (No.10 Orleans Road) was listed as a school in 1899. By 1900/01, the years in question, it was no longer a school, but listed in *Kelly's Directory* as a *'Dancing academy'.* The first reference to the premises becoming an engineering workshop was in 1905/6, when it was occupied by Dignus Engineering Co. Of course, street directories were not always reliable or up to date.

The wide acceptance of the Orleans Road works as the company's first location is highly unlikely, looking at the evidence. It is more likely that during the 1920s, a period of growing interest in 'veteran' cars, that the Orleans name was taken by motoring writers to suggest a location in Orleans Road. By that time there was a long established engineering works on the corner with Chapel Road and by 1928, No.12 King Street no longer existed (demolished to widen King Street). When Tamplin was writing his letters", it may already have become accepted, even locally, that the *Orleans* Works had been in *Orleans* Road, as the name would appear to suggest.

The evidence points to central Twickenham as the first location for the company as Tamplin recalls. An 1898 advertisement *(fig 29)* for HG Burford & Co describes No.12 King Street (*'opposite the bank'*) as the *'Orleans Works'*. Interestingly, *Kelly's Directory* shows that in 1900/01 one of the occupants listed there was the *'Mechanical Construction Co., engineers'*[(13)], suggesting car construction at No.12, probably the

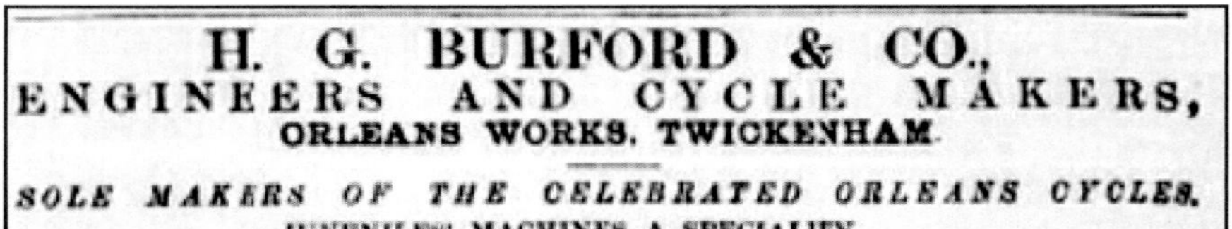

Fig 29

Fig 30

company was set up by Burford and van Toll. The photograph *(fig 30)* shows the rear of No.12 King Street a little later, advertising *'Motor, Cycle & General engineers'* and *'Motor Experts'. C. Heal'* blacksmith next door, in Pound Lane between Cross Deep and Wharf Lane, marked *'Smithy'* on the 1907 Goad map *(see fig 17)*.

However, there is another possibility. On 25th December 1898, Burford and van Toll had also taken out a lease on premises at No.10 Heath Road, almost opposite 12 King Street. Perhaps this had been taken in readiness for finding a suitable car already in production elsewhere, that could be built under license in Twickenham. It was on the north side of Heath Road with a yard behind, so offering the possibility of workshop space. It seems that this may also have been used as a works, sharing in the construction process of the New Orleans cars until the new factory, almost behind, was ready. The Goad map shows both premises and the Orleans motor works between Holly Place and Sherland Road, marked *'Orleans Motor Co. Ltd.'*, not only built but already extended by 1907. No.12 King Street is marked *'Cycles'*, bottom right *(see fig 17)*, No.10 Heath Road (by then renumbered No.20) is shown as *'Vac(ant) May'07'* with a *'Motor Car Upholster'* behind, facing Holly Road, marked *'Avenue'* (Avenue Cottages) on the map. So there is also the possibility

34

that the car upholstery works could previously have been a small car works, immediately behind No.10. This works may have been connected with '*Mrs Giles & Son Coach builder*' recorded at No.12 (later numbered No.26) Heath Road in 1901/02 [13].

The *Motor-Car Journal* dated 3rd February 1900 records that ten Voiturettes were in stock... '*at the New Orleans Works, where there is already a very nice little plant... while in rear of the present premises a large area of land... has been obtained on a long lease*'. This appears to be a reference to No.10 Heath Road and the site for the new factory almost behind.

The aerial photograph referred to earlier *(see fig 18)* of the Cross Deep junction with King Street before it was widened, shows No.12 King Street clearly visible in the foreground (bottom right). The former Orleans Works is towards the top left of the photograph and and No.10 (later numbered No.20) Heath Road is also visible (centre bottom). The photograph of No.10 Heath Road *(fig 31)* was taken a few years later when it had become Tamplin's Garage renumbered as 20. Cecil Tamplin can be seen standing at the entrance.

Fig 31

No.10 Heath Road is mentioned in a document dated 22nd March 1901 [14], as were premises between Holly Place and Sherland Road, the site for the new purpose-built factory. Interestingly, land on Eel Pie Island is also listed, probably related to van Toll's continuing work with motorboats. There is no mention of a works in Orleans Road.

As early as the January 1900 article in *The Motorcar Journal*, it was reported that '*Messrs Burford, Van toll and Co... in addition to their present factory, being engaged on the construction of a new works 200 feet long by 60 feet wide... equipped with the most modern machine tools*'. [4] More workshop space would have been required in 1900 with the manufacture of the Voiturette in relatively large numbers with - '*operations now in hand on the construction of a first lot of 100 of this type of car*' [4]. At this point they may have rented further premises (though unlikely to be at Orleans Road) whilst waiting for the factory to be completed between Holly Place and Sherland Road.

It is clear from the 1901 census that the new works was ready to open by 31st March 1901, Census Day. Walter Hagreen is recorded as '*caretaker to the Orleans Motor Car Co. Ltd.*', living at the premises with his family. A newspaper report from 1901 quotes the foreman of the works, Ernest Coxhead, saying that the Orleans Motor Co. '*were in the new premises (by) about April this year*' (presumably 1901) [15]. Holly Place became the company's registered address on 21st September 1901. The opening of the new works should have provided sufficient space to construct the rest of the 600 Voiturettes produced in the first two years of production. There is evidence of further expansion of the works in a planning application dated May 1903, [16] (see Appendix VI).

Following the collapse of the company, the Orleans works closed in 1910.

No.12 King Street remained a cycle works and was still listed as the Orleans Cycle Co. in Kelly's Directory for 1905/6 and the disputed Orleans Road Works on the corner of Orleans and Chapel Roads had become an engineering works by 1905/6 (as mentioned earlier). The building has survived and remains remarkably unchanged from when it was built, as the photographs taken in 2018 show (*figs 32a and 32b*).

Fig 32a

Fig 32b

However, the end of Orleans cars was by no means the end of motor manufacturing in the town. A workforce of skilled motor engineers was now looking for work and new car makers were emerging or being attracted to Twickenham.

4. Johannes van Toll: Twickenham's

MOTORING PIONEER

IN THE LATE 1880s, Dutch engineer Johannes van Toll was working with Gottlieb Daimler in Germany on his innovative *'high-speed'* petrol engine. Before joining Daimler, van Toll had been superintendent at a factory where the engine was used to drive a chocolate compressing machine, one of the engine's earliest uses. Van Toll was one of the earliest pioneers of the internal-combustion engine.

Not long after, van Toll came to England as Frederick Simms' chief engineer and moved to Twickenham and to No.13, Heathfield South, Twickenham, to be closer to Simms' Eel Pie Island base. Now known as *John* van Toll, he moved to 58, Whitton Road, Twickenham. He called his house Villa Roosendaal after his Dutch hometown. The photograph *(fig 33)* shows John van Toll and his wife Florence with their two sons, Thomas and John, c1900.

Fig 33

In June 1895, Simms' friend Evelyn Ellis had bought a Panhard-Levassor motorcar in Paris. On 5th July 1895, Ellis and Simms drove from the village of Micheldever Station in Hampshire to Datchet, a distance of 56 miles, thus completing the first long-distance car journey in Britain. The journey took five and a half hours and was breaking the law but helped pave the way

Fig 34

for the partial repeal of the 1865 Locomotive Act (known as the 'Red-Flag Act') though not the Act altogether. The Act was finally replaced altogether by the Motor Car Act in 1903. Van Toll's family maintain that Johannes accompanied them on the journey as driver/mechanic. There is, however, no evidence for this and the claim has been dismissed by a number of motoring writers.

On the first weekend in July each year, the Ellis veteran car journey is re-enacted with 40 or more pre-1905 cars and motorcycles making the same journey. The photograph *(fig 34)* shows Ellis at the wheel the Panhard-Levessor at a motor show held at Tunbridge Wells on 15th October 1895. The gentleman in the top hat behind him, thought to be van Toll, was in fact, James Critchley.

In 1896 Simms and motoring entrepreneur Harry Lawson organised the Emancipation Run from London to Brighton to celebrate the demise of the Red Flag Act. Johannes van Toll drove the German Daimler Landau named *'Modern Times'*, shown in the photograph *(fig 35)*, with Gottlieb Daimler, Wilhelm Maybach and Frederick Simms as passengers. Quite a team: Daimler and Maybach, inventors of the Daimler engine, went on to form the companies that became Mercedes-Benz; Simms became

Fig 35

known as *'the father of the British motor industry'* [1] and van Toll was responsible for Twickenham's first motorcar.

Seventeen cars made it to Brighton, led by an American built Duryea brought over from the States to take part. This was the first time American cars had been seen in Europe. In recent years, around 500 cars have taken part in the London to Brighton Veteran Car Run. It has been run almost every year since 1927 to commemorate the 1896 Emancipation Run. The *Daily Sketch* newspaper first sponsored the event and dubbed it *'The Old Crocks Run'*. All competing cars must have been built before 1905. It is the world's longest running motoring event.

Also in 1896 van Toll and his friend Otto Mayer, with whom he later went into business in Twickenham, accompanied Simms to the Daimler factory in Cannstatt, Germany. They had gone to select engines that could be used in the British Daimler operation. They chose the V-twin engine, partly because Simms wanted to use it in his river launches. Van Toll was to develop new 4 hp and 8 hp horizontal-engined launches on

Eel Pie Island. This particular project was apparently unsuccessful. Nevertheless, van Toll signed a three-year contract with the newly established Daimler Motor Co. in January the following year. He was to continue building river launches on Eel Pie Island on a salary of £225 pa [17].

Van Toll was contracted to work for Simms until January 1900 even though Daimler was moving its manufacturing base to Coventry. It appears that by October 1897 van Toll was at the Coventry factory and involved in the acceptance trials of Evelyn Ellis's new *'dos-a-dos'* bodied Daimler *'specially built for touring both at home and abroad'* [18]. The car was rather optimistically referred to as the *'Alpine'* model.

With Daimler's Eel Pie Island operation at an end, van Toll was keen to get into motorcar manufacturing. Once back in Twickenham he continued building motorboats on Eel Pie Island, while making plans to build cars nearby taking advantage of the team of skilled motor engineers he'd built up on the island.

During 1899, even though still contracted to Simms, van Toll teamed up with Henry Burford and F. A. Rodewald, to build cars in Twickenham, as described in Chapter 3. The company started marketing the New Orleans Voiturette in January of the following year, when van Toll's contract with Simms had expired. Van Toll was now also building motorboats with Henry Burford, as reported in *The Highland News*, July 1900, which mentions *'a Mr E. Cleaver of Burford & Van Toll piloting a clinker built motor pinnace on Loch Ness'*, which was a Daimler engined motorboat built by Paul Jones & Son of Gourock. By October 1905, van Toll had teamed up with another former Daimler colleague, Otto Mayer, to form Maytoll motor and marine engineers in Richmond Road. *'Van Toll, Mayer & Co., Motor Engineers'* can be seen in the c1907 photograph *(fig 36a)* with the same view over 110 years later *(fig 36b)*.

A report in the *Sportsman* dated 26th November 1909 appears to suggest that, while the Orleans Motor Company was winding down its motor car production, it might have been returning to its nautical roots. Another report states that Britain was trying to retake the British International

Figs 36a and 36b

Cup, a boat race, which the Americans had held since 1907: *'the challengers on this occasion, the British Motor Boat Club, who will be represented by a forty-footer constructed by the Orleans Motor Company of Twickenham... which will shake American motor boating up!'* [19]. However, it seems more likely that these reports were confusing the Orleans Motor Company with Van Toll, Mayer & Co., Motor Engineers. The *'Van Toll, Mayer and Co., Motor Engineers'* business card *(fig 37)* mentions both *'motor cars'* and *'motor launches'*. It seems likely that it was van Toll's new company that was the link between the Orleans Motor

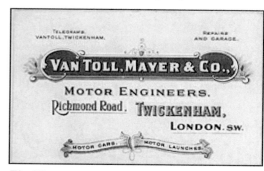

Fig 37

Company and the British Motor Boat Club. Although van Toll had been involved in the manufacture of New Orleans cars until at least 1903, he'd had little involvement in the Orleans cars that followed.

The premises in Richmond Road are still there, as the

Fig 38

2018 photograph *(fig 38)* shows and was known as Orleans Garage for many years - still a motor engineers and garage, over 100 years later. Thomas Jenner owned Orleans Garage from 1916 until his death in 1929. After leaving the Orleans company when it closed in 1910, he opened his first garage at No.10 Heath Road. This premises had previously been leased by Burford and Van Toll. It later became Tamplin's Garage (see Chapter 9). His son Thomas continued to run Orleans Garage until 1965. At the time of the photograph Alan Fox was the proprietor and had researched Orleans cars when he took over the premises. His office looked as if it had hardly changed in over 100 years. The walls were lined with photographs of Orleans cars, some taken at the Isle of Man TT. Also hanging there was the Certificate of Performance for the Orleans car *(see fig 19)* shown in Chapter 3.

By 1909, van Toll was dipping his toe into the fledgling aircraft industry. He established Erade and Van Toll in Twickenham and at the same time renewing his association with the Belgian motor manufacturer Vivinus (as the poster *(fig 39)* shows). What, if any, success this venture may have had, is unclear but it was not to be long lasting, as by 1912 Vivinus had gone into liquidation, followed by van Toll's untimely death in 1913, aged just fifty-two. *'John'* van Toll is buried in Twickenham Cemetery with his wife Florence and their son John. His headstone is shown in the photograph *(fig 40)* taken in January 2021.

Fig 39

Fig 40

5. Not just cars ... buses too

AT THE SAME time as the Orleans cars were being built in central Twickenham, two companies building buses moved into premises not far away. They would have been attracted to Twickenham by the growing number of experienced motor engineers and coach builders. Both companies would also have wanted a manufacturing base close to London, in order to supply buses to the London General Omnibus Co. (LGOC), which had started using motor buses in 1902.

Beaufort Motor Company

The Beaufort Motor Co. designed a twin-cylinder 12 hp petrol lorry in 1904, and a 10-12 hp and a 24 hp motorcar in 1905. Beaufort exhibited lorries, buses and cars at the 1905 Olympia Motor Exhibition as the advertisement *(fig 41)* shows. At about that time they started to build motor vehicles at the Beaufort Works in Beaufort Road, East Twickenham. The Beaufort Engineering Works, shown on the map *(fig 42)*, was constructed on the site of the Roseneath Stables, directly adjoining Marble Hill Park.

Although registered in London, Beaufort had its

Fig 41

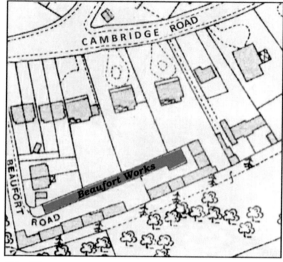

Fig 42

manufacturing base in Baden, Germany. Chassis, engines and mechanical components, as in the photograph *(fig 43)*, may have come from Germany to have coachwork fitted in Twickenham.

The LGOC did try out a few Beaufort buses - open-top double-deckers with chain drive. However, the LGOC decided against buying them, choosing instead to build their own buses. First, they built the X type in 1909 followed by the iconic B type in 1910, which is considered to be the first mass-produced motor bus. Not many Beaufort vehicles were sold and the Beaufort Motor Co. soon went out of business.

The company may have had connections with Henry Burford who set up the National Omnibus Company in the early 1900s.

Meanwhile, a mile or so away on the other side of Twickenham, Scott, Stirling had become established for the same reasons as the Beaufort Motor Company. Initially Scott, Stirling had much more success than Beaufort building motor buses in Twickenham.

Fig 43

Scott, Stirling & Co. Ltd.

John Stirling had first built Daimler powered motorcars in Hamilton, Lanarkshire from 1897 before moving into commercial vehicles. He would have had contact with Simms in Twickenham, to obtain the Daimler engines. There is no evidence of Stirling cars being made in Twickenham despite the 1908 Post Office directory listing of the company as *'A Motor Car Makers'*.

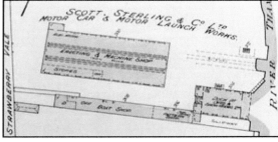

Fig 44

The site of the Stirling Motor Works in Twickenham appears initially to have been the *'Works'* on Swan Island and the larger island that existed at that time, behind No.1 Strawberry Vale (see Chapter 9). *'Scott, Stirling Motor Carriages Ltd'* was listed in Kelly's Directory at the site in 1903/4. With the size of the vehicles and the planned scale of production, a new *'Motor Car and Motor Launch Works'* was built a little further up Strawberry Vale by 1907, as the Goad map *(fig 44)* shows. The 1907 Goad map also shows that they had premises a few hundred yards upstream, on Manor Road, apparently used as a *'Store'* on the right of the map *(fig 45)*. It is the same building that would be used by Monarch Motor Co, as a boathouse and workshop,

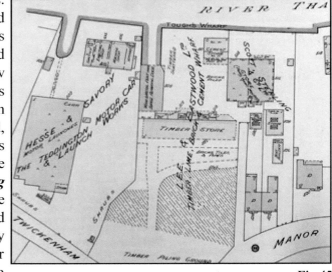

Fig 45

shown in the photograph in Chapter 8 *(see fig 98)* and now 'The Wharf' restaurant. The Teddington Motor Car and Launch Works on Twickenham Road is to left of the map (Chapter 8). Although it is possible that the coachwork for Scott, Stirling omnibuses may have been built at the works, it is more likely that it was built by one of a number of local coach builders.

John Stirling claimed, in 1896, to have been the first person in the UK to inaugurate a motor bus service. Stirling also claimed, in an interview reported in *The Financial Times,* to have made the first serious attempt to organise a bus service in London in 1901. The London Power Omnibus Co. had by 1903 built up a fleet of over 70 Scott, Stirling double-deckers. An article in *The Daily Telegraph & Courie*r on 12th December 1905 recorded that an order for 100 Scott, Stirling buses for the *'London Power Omnibus Co. Ltd.'* was ... *'the largest order yet placed with any British omnibus manufacturer'.* The photograph *(fig 46)* shows a Scott, Stirling Pioneer bus advertising *'Scott, Stirling, Twickenham',* exhibited at *'The Olympia Show'*, commercial motors section, in 1905. As part of the promise that their buses were *'designed for long life',* they offered to maintain them for ten years at a flat rate. The photograph *(fig 47)* shows a Twickenham built Scott, Stirling double-decker en route to Cricklewood. The buses were operated by Power Omnibus Co. under the Pioneer name from their Cricklewood headquarters and depot. London bus companies adopted names for their services that suggested greater speed or superiority over their rivals. As well as Pioneer, names like Arrow, Vanguard and Rapide were used.

Fig 46

Fig 47

Fig 48

In addition to the double-decker with 16 seats inside and 18 seats outside on the upper deck, a single-decker with 18 seats was offered by Scott, Stirling. Both had a four-cylinder 24 hp petrol engine described as having *'each cylinder cast separately'* [20]. The photograph *(fig 48)* shows a passenger disembarking from a Scott, Stirling single-decker at the Rosapenna Hotel in Donegal. The company would also appear to have had some success exporting their products, with sales to several countries including India, South Africa, Canada and Argentina. Scott, Stirling also offered *'all types of commercial motors'* [21] that were *'British built throughout'*.

Scott, Stirling's success as a motor manufacturer was short lived. By the end of 1907 the company was being wound-up and a liquidator appointed. There appear to have been problems of reliability with their buses. As one of the pioneering motor-bus manufacturers in the country, the problem of reliability was seized upon by horse-bus operators. In October 1908, a *'sale of the plant, machinery and stock'* was held at the *'Thameside Works'*, which interestingly included *'Modern Motor Launches and Boats'* [22]. Scott, Stirling would also appear to have manufactured motor boats.

How many Scott, Stirling buses were eventually built is unknown and no buses or motor launches appear to have survived.

By 1908, the dominance of the London General Omnibus Company (LGOC) saw the majority of small bus operators go out of business or taken over by the LGOC. By 1909, LGOC had started to manufacture its own buses.

6. TWICKENHAM VEHICLES BEFORE AND JUST AFTER WORLD WAR 1

THE FAILURE OF the Beaufort and Scott, Stirling operations, followed by the collapse of the Orleans company in 1910, didn't signal the end of Twickenham's motor industry. New car makers were becoming established in new locations around the borough as well as taking over the vacated motor works and, doubtless, the trained local workforce.

Following the success of the New Orleans Voiturette and failure of the larger and more expensive Orleans cars, car makers establishing in Twickenham concentrated on smaller, lighter vehicles. At the time, these were becoming known as 'cycle cars' and 'light cars'. Light cars, as the name suggests, were smaller, simpler and cheaper cars aimed at the less well-off aspiring motorist. They started to appear on the market around 1910 and were seen as a step up from the very basic cycle cars appearing on the market at that time, like the AV Monocar, explored in Chapter 8.

During the 1914-18 war, most engineering companies switched to making military machinery and weapons. After the war had ended some motor companies picked up where they left off, producing the same models or developing new models. Others shifted to commercial vehicle production or disappeared from the market altogether. Unfortunately this return to motorcar production was to be short lived and almost all motor manufacturing had stopped in Twickenham by 1926.

Corben's Carriage factory and Twickenham Motor Co.

The Corben brothers, Charles and Ben, opened a carriage factory on the corner of Richmond Road and Oak Lane in 1852. The map *(fig 49)* dating from c1894 shows a substantial building marked *'Carriage factory'*. This was before York Street had been constructed to link the Richmond Road with King Street by-passing Church Street in 1899. The photograph

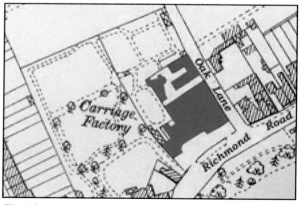

Fig 49

(fig 50) shows the Corben Carriage Factory in the late 19th century with a number of carriages under construction and the royal coat of arms above the name board. Charles Corben also had premises prominently placed on the corner of Cross Deep and Heath Road. When Charles retired, the Heath Road premises closed and Ben continued in Richmond Road until his untimely death in 1902.

By the 1900s, Corben's were constructing the bodywork for all types of vehicles. They built the coachwork for the GWR *'observation car'* shown in the photograph *(fig 51)*. This charabanc (small open motor coach) was built in 1905, seated 16 passengers and carried luggage on the roof. Corben Brothers factory in Richmond Road was also referred to as a *'Carriage and Motor Car Factory'* on Goad's map of May 1907 *(fig 52)*. The company remained on the site as Corben's until at least 1908, according to *Kelly's Directory*.

Fig 50

The skills and experience of carriage builders were utilised by Twickenham's car makers. The Orleans cars of 1905 until 1910 had elaborate coachwork and probably turned to the former Carriage Factory for their coachwork. By c1911, Twickenham Motor Company was established at the site. The photograph *(fig 53)* of a car with coachwork by Twickenham Motor Co. Ltd. appears to have been built on an Orleans chassis of the period looking at the radiator shape and style. The

Fig 51

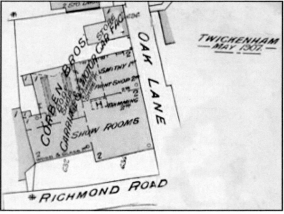

Fig 52

Fig 53

Fig 54

Fig 55

photograph *(fig 54)* shows the Lyric Palace cinema with Twickenham Motor Company next door. Two cars of the period can be seen outside and a sign offering 'Cars for Hire'. The aerial photograph *(fig 55)* shows the Lyric Palace cinema and the motor works at about the same period.

Wyvern Light Cars

The advertisement *(fig 56)* for the Wyvern gives the company's name as Wyvern Light Cars with its address at 9-11, Richmond Road and the advertisement *(fig 57)* from 1914 describes the Twickenham Motor Company as *'Automobile Carriage Builders'* at the same address. It is likely that the company was involved in building the Wyvern. The Wyvern was an early example of the cheaper light cars that were coming on to the market. It had a 10.5 hp 4 cylinder engine made by Chapuis-Dornier in Puteaux, near Paris.

Fig 56

Fig 57

The Wyvern was only produced in 1913 and 1914 and was fitted with a three-speed gearbox and shaft drive. With a two-seater body, it had a distinctive V-shaped radiator similar to the much larger L'Auto Metallurgique cars being produced in Belgium. There are no records of how many Wyvern cars were produced and no car or commercial vehicle made at the site appears to have survived.

The Twickenham Motor Company continued at the site until 1916, when it went into liquidation.

Palladium Autocars and Autovan

Kelly's Directory lists Palladium Autocars at 11, Richmond Road, in 1913. Palladian Autocars had been making cars since 1912 in Felsham Road, Putney according to Grace's Guide. It is possible that they were using part of this large site as a showroom or to build the coachwork for their *'handsome Berliner limousine'* [8] and the delivery

wagon they were also marketing at the time. Grace's Guide also confirms that Palladium produced *'Petrol Motor Commercial Vehicles'* from 1913. The photograph *(fig 58)* shows an Autovan commercial vehicle of the period.

Fig 58

In 1914, Autovan was recorded at the address, which suggests that Palladium's commercial vehicle coach building was now based at the site. Autovan remained there during and after the First World War as a *'vehicle manufacturers in Richmond Road'* [23], manufacturing or at least constructing the bodywork for commercial vehicles until the early 1920s. Palladium closed in 1924, like so many other local motor manufacturers.

At least one Palladium car is known to have survived, but no Autovans.

By 1920 A.W. Bradbury & Co. Ltd., motor engineers, had become established at the Richmond Road site as the c1925 photograph *(fig 59)* shows. As well as servicing and hiring out cars, Bradbury's seems likely to have continued constructing the coachwork for motor vehicles, including charabancs. Initially, they shared the premises with Autovan but by 1922 they appear to be the only motor company registered at the site.

Fig 59

Disaster struck at Bradbury's in 1926. At 4am one Tuesday in August, a huge storm struck Twickenham. Two hours after the storm had passed, a police constable noticed, through the showroom window, a charabanc on

Fig 60

fire. Firemen battled for two hours and successfully prevented the fire from reaching the fuel storage tanks. However the building was totally destroyed, as the photograph *(fig 60)* shows, along with 36 motor vehicles including two charabancs, causing £40,000 worth of damage. The fire was believed to have been started by a lightning strike. The factory and garage were later demolished.

Twickenham Kinema was built on the former Corben's site in 1928, after the burnt-out remains of the carriage factory were demolished. The cinema was renamed the Queen's cinema in 1940 and then the Gaumont in 1950. However, after the Gaumont itself was demolished in 1958, the site returned much closer to its roots as a Spikins of Twickenham garage. The photograph *(fig 61)* shows Spikins Garage in January 1968. The roof of the old Lyric Palace cinema can be seen behind.[24] The Spikins' site still maintains its motoring connection (2024), as Oak Lane petrol station.

Fig 61

Another part of Twickenham to become associated with motor engineering was to the north of Twickenham Green. Cycle making and coach building were already established there before the First World War, when the Medina Engineering Co. Ltd started to produce motorcars in Gould Road. The 1915 map *(fig 62)* shows the Engineering Works in Gould Road near Twickenham Green.

Mercury Cars Ltd.

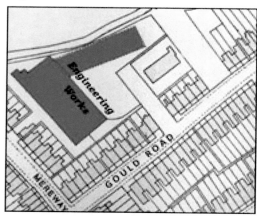

Fig 62

The Mercury was another of the early light cars, with a 10 hp engine, two seats and selling at £190. It was described as a *'large car in miniature'*. Medina started production of the Mercury in 1914 but by 1916, like other engineering firms, had turned to the supply of munitions and military hardware for the First World War. The company reappeared in 1919 with a new name: Mercury Cars Ltd. and a new address in May Road just round the corner from Gould Road.

The Mercury 10 hp two-seater reappeared and was shown at the 1919 Olympia Motor Show. The photograph of the car shown in Mercury Cars' advertisement *(fig 63)* of 1919 was taken at the end of May Road with Twickenham Green and Holy Trinity Church in the background.

The 10 hp 2-seater was one of the most elegant light cars on the market as the photograph *(fig 64)* shows. It had a 1298 cc four-cylinder Medina-Hastings engine made at their own factory. The price, however, had risen to £375.

The coachwork for Mercury cars may have been built at the factory but was more likely built by coach builders locally, in common with other car makers in this period. Established coach builder W. H. Arnold chose the Mercury chassis for their all-weather two-door *Eclipse* coupe. They displayed this very handsome, and sizeable looking (for a light car*) 'luxury'*

Fig 63

saloon car at the 1919 Motor Show. This advertisement *(fig 65)* shows the W. H. Arnold & Co. Eclipse bodied Mercury car. W. H. Arnold were probably best known for supplying the coachwork for specialist Rolls Royce and Bentley cars.

Fig 64

"Quality" Motor Coach Work

The "Eclipse" Allweather Body

W.H.ARNOLD&CO

31, YORK PLACE, PORTMAN SQUARE, W.1

Fig 65

Mercury Cars also had a splendid bonnet mascot depicting the Roman god Mercury 'The Messenger', shown in the photograph *(fig 66)* taken from an advertisement for the 1920 Mercury two-seater model. This mascot does not appear in the photographs of the 1919 model.

A new Mercury model with a larger 1794cc engine joined the range in 1920. Mercury had produced over 200 cars by this point. However, production was soon to come to an end as Mercury Cars Ltd. became another victim of the large mass-producers like Ford. Production had ceased completely by 1923.

No Mercury cars appear to have survived.

Twickenham was at the forefront of the light car boom, which attracted other potential light-car manufacturers to Twickenham. The skilled local labour force and proximity to the London market, would again have been factors. John Bernard Taunton, who had worked for Charles Rolls, built his first 8 hp advanced light car in Twickenham. Drawings were completed in July 1912 for a car with a *'one-piece'* structure applied to the chassis and engine. The underslung chassis incorporated parts of the engine into a single stamping, described as *'like a metal punt'* [25]. The car was later described as *'too far ahead of its time'* [25].

Fig 66

60

Taunton Cars Ltd.

The first experimental car, seen in the photograph *(fig 67)*, was built between 2nd September and 12th November 1912, in Twickenham. It seems that a chassis was tested with six adults and 5 cwt of ballast over some 8000 miles. Four prototypes were built of the lightweight but well-equipped two-seater and four-seater models, shown in the photograph *(fig 68)*. The Taunton engine *(fig 69)* was *'an advanced design for 1912...a neat 14.4hp overhead-inlet, side-exhaust... single casting'.* [25]

Fig 67

Fig 68

Fig 69

An initial production of 2,400 cars was negotiated from two factories in Scotland. The location of Taunton's workshop in Twickenham where the production cars were built, is unclear. The 1914 Taunton brochure was produced in readiness. The cover shown *(fig 70)*, evoked the romance of the road. The car's greyhound mascot came from Taunton's family crest. Interestingly the company saw *'the lady driver'* as an important market.

The deal however fell through and it was decided to build a new factory near London, possibly in Twickenham. But a factory was required

Fig 70

immediately, already up and running, in order to start production and to keep investors happy. A vacant and fully equipped motor factory was located in Belgium, the Hermes factory near Liege. But bad luck hit after only a handful of cars had been built. The German army advanced into Belgium and production was halted.

Attempts were made to restart production after the war but with apparently limited success. The 1917 *Red Book of Motor Car and Cycle Car Manufacturers*, shows that 191 Taunton two-seater four-cylinder 14 hp cars were produced in Belgium. However, The A-Z of Cars of the 1920s by Nick Baldwin states that *'a few two-seat cars'* were produced in 1919-20, possibly in Twickenham. Exactly how many Taunton cars were eventually made and where they were made remains unclear.

The Taunton seems to have been a great Twickenham designed and developed car that never achieved its potential.

The Lington Engineering Co. Ltd.

In 1920, another light car appeared on the scene in Twickenham, advertised as... *'for the light car connoisseur'*. The address shown on the Lington advertisement *(fig 71)*, is 61, London Road, Twickenham. The site was approximately where Moore's Cycles is today and can be seen in the photographs *(figs 72a and 72b)* on the right, which was at the time W&S Lewis 'Electrical and General Engineers'. The address may have been a showroom and a workshop. Lingtons were apparently made at the Grosvenor Works in Bedford, mentioned as their works in advertisements. This was probably where the chassis and V-twin cylinder 10 hp engine were made, to be fitted with coachwork built in Twickenham. The Lington, or Elfin, as it was previously known, were very much in the mould of other light cars made in Twickenham, with a

Fig 71

V-twin cylinder 10 hp engine. One notable feature was the floor mounted pedal used to start the car. The Lington went into production in 1920.

It is not known how many were made, over what period or if any have survived.

It was not only light car manufacturers that were attracted to Twickenham. Two well established motor manufacturers came to the town, not just to build cars but also heavy commercial vehicles: Straker-Squire and the French Berliet company.

Straker-Squire manufactured commercial vehicle including lorries, buses and ambulances in addition to motorcars. The company also built Rolls-Royce Falcon aero engines under licence. Their head office was in

Fig 72a

Fig 72b, below

London but their factory had been located at Fishponds near Bristol and, after Twickenham, in Angel Road, Edmonton.

When Orleans Cars went into liquidation in 1910 the company vacated the motor works situated between Holly Place and Sherland Road. In January 1914 Straker-Squire needed to acquire additional manufacturing facilities and bought the site. They re-equipped the factory with the latest machinery and automatic, labour-saving tooling, before transferring their motor manufacturing operation to Twickenham. The February 1914 advertisement *(fig 73)* for Straker-Squire's *'World's Best'* 15-20 hp car gives their Shaftesbury Avenue address. However the April 1916 advertisement in *The Motor Trader*, *(fig 74)* for 4 and 5 ton *'high class'* trucks, already supplied to the government, gives the Sherland Road, Twickenham address. Their Bristol works was by then completely given over to the production of munitions, so the company's vehicle production moved to Twickenham.

Straker-Squire Ltd.

Once established in Twickenham in 1915, Straker-Squire were advertising in the press for *'motor component'* machine-tool operators and *'experienced fitters for motor lorry chassis construction'*. The *Globe* newspaper reported in March 1915 that *'... the Twickenham workshop increased their revenue to the extent of £90,000. They had two departments - the pleasure car ... and industrial departments'*.

Although the outbreak of war had *'affected pleasure car sales'*, Straker-Squire

Fig 73

expected that demand would grow, with the war anticipated to end in the autumn of 1915. They would be ready in 1916 to launch a *'new model car'* that would have *'the best of everything a motorcar could possess'* [(26)].

Straker-Squire Motorcars had a striking bonnet ornament that may have been inspired by Rolls Royce's iconic *'Spirit of Ecstasy'* or *'Flying Lady'*. The latter had been sculpted by Charles Sykes for Baron Montagu of Beaulieu's own 1909 Rolls Royce Silver Ghost. Intriguingly, it was an expression of Beaulieu's secret

Fig 74

passion for Eleanor Thornton, who was a model for the Flying Lady. She later appeared on the bonnet of all Rolls-Royce cars. The

photograph *(fig 75a)* shows the kneeling Spirit of Ecstasy used on the Rolls Royce Phantom IV. The Straker-Squire kneeling girl bonnet mascot, is shown in the photographs *(figs 75b/c)*, side view and driver's view. The photograph *(fig 76)* of a Straker-Squire 6-cylinder cars shows the characteristic radiator mascot.

In the event, the First World War didn't end in 1915 and at some point the works was also given over to munitions production, like Staker-Squire's other factories. Interestingly, in September 1916, the British government proposed taking over the factory to train desperately needed munitions workers. The target was to train 400 metal and engineering workers every four weeks or so in what was the first such training centre in the country. The photograph *(fig 77)* suggests that they were training a predominantly female workforce. *'Munitions Workers, Straker-Squire, Sherland Road, Twickenham'* is written on the back of the photo, dated February 1917. This may have been one training cohort's 'end of course' photograph. The factory is also believed to have been used as a training and rehabilitation centre for wounded and disabled servicemen after the end of the First World War.

Straker-Squire sold their Bristol factory making aero engines to the American company Cosmos, in 1919. They also decided to sell the Twickenham factory the same year and all cars and commercial vehicle production moved to Edmonton in 1920.

Figs 75a, 75b and 75c

Fig 76

Fig 77

A small number of Straker-Squire vehicles have survived. It is not known if any of them were constructed in Twickenham.

Interestingly, *Kelly's Directory* confirms that The Orleans Motor Co. Ltd. was at the Sherland Road works until 1910, but no other entries for the site are recorded until 1923. The site was however used, for example, by the Brompton Motor company which used the works as a car repair depot c1913. Part of the reason for the lack of records may have been for national security - the site was being used for heavy vehicle construction for the war effort and later as a government training centre. By 1920, the site appears to have become an *'Aero engines Instructional Works'* for the Ministry of Munitions [27] and the Ministry of Labour in 1923. No other occupants are recorded until the site was bought by The Poppe Rubber and Tyre Co. Ltd in 1927.

August and Frederick Poppe, German born rubber dealers, had set up the company locally in 1911. As the company name suggests, it was making items, principally tyres and rubber components, for the motor industry. By the 1930s they were also making components for the aircraft industry. Poppe Rubber remained at the site until shortly before the buildings were demolished in the late 1980s. The site can seen from Sherland Road in the photographs *(figs 78a/b/c)*. It is now a car park. The original wall with two gateways do however remain intact, as the photographs show.

Berliet Motor and Engineering Co. Ltd.

The Berliet company started making motorcars in 1899 near Lyons in France.

By 1921, a British branch of Berliet was formed with a London office in Sackville Street. The advertisement *(fig 79)* shows the 1909 Berliet model on offer through their London agents. A motor works was opened in Westminster Bridge Road and

Figs 78a, 78b and 78c

Fig 79

Lower Marsh, Waterloo and a car service and repair depot in Cambridge Road, East Twickenham. The Twickenham depot became known as the Richmond Bridge Works, where vehicles were later assembled as well as serviced. The depot was part of the former Pelabon Munitions site.

Berliet manufactured motor vehicles at the Richmond Bridge Works in Cambridge Road between 1925 and 1930. The Works is shown on the map *(fig 80)*, close to Richmond Ice Rink. In 1927, the British company trialled a prototype two-seater taxi. By 1929, the Richmond Bridge Works was offering a range of six models of Berliet cars, including the Junior Six.

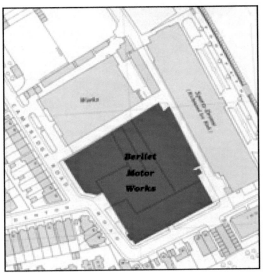

Fig 80

Berliet in France had moved into commercial vehicle construction during the First World War. This later became their main activity. The 1930 advertisement *(fig 81)* for the Berliet company offers a range of trucks suggesting that commercial vehicle production was now taking place in Cambridge Road.

Fig 81

Fig 82

Berliet also marketed a 'medium sized' bus in 1927, [28] a one-man operated 20 seater *(fig 82)*. It seems likely that French Berliet chassis arrived at the works for assembly and were then fitted with one of a range of commercial bodies. The closure of the works not very long after would suggest that this enterprise was not a success. The premises remained empty until becoming home to Wright Brothers Removals and later Bishops Move.

The Berliet company continued to produce commercial vehicles in France until 1980, under Citroen's ownership from 1967.

A number of Berliet vehicles have survived but it is not known whether any were constructed in Twickenham.

7. TWICKENHAM'S MOTORBIKES

DURING THE 1920s Twickenham became something of a centre for motorcycle manufacturing. The industry was centred mainly around St.Margarets, on the eastern side of the borough. The most notable of the Twickenham motorcycle marques was the Grigg. Grigg started building motor scooters aimed at the less well off, much like the local motorcar makers who were having success in that market at the time. Grigg went on to develop a wide range of motorcycles including larger machines that were fitted with sidecars. The motorcycle and sidecar was a much cheaper form of family motoring for those who could not afford to buy or run a motorcar.

Argson Engineering at the Beaufort works, added to the range of motor vehicle produced locally, with their three-wheeler 'invalid carriages'. These later became important for AC Cars on the other side of the borough (see Chapter 8).

Grigg Motorcycles

Grigg was established in 1920 by Harry Grigg at the Winchester Works in Winchester Road, St. Margarets *(fig 83)*. Initially small motor scooters were made with 1.75 hp 2-stroke engines, like the one in the photograph

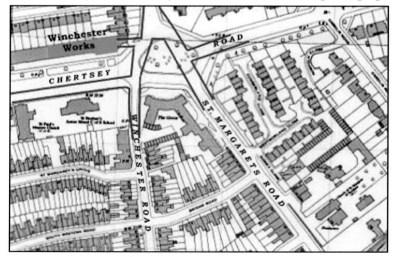

Fig 83

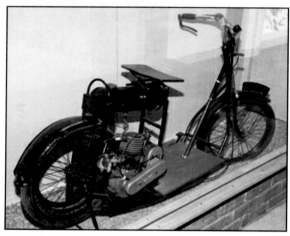

(fig 84). 'As docile as any power propelled vehicle… undoubtedly the type which should be used by the girl, lady or elderly gentleman'.[29] But demand for motor scooters was declining, so in 1921 a 162 cc lightweight motorcycle was launched. A three-speed version followed in the following year.

Fig 84

By 1923, the company was building a range of much larger machines under the banner *'Grigg - the hallmark of excellence in Engineering'*[30]. The Winchester Works was expanded into *'one of the most modern Motor Cycle Factories in the world'*, according to Grigg's own promotional material. The range now included three single-cylinder models, the Ajax, the Zeus and the Mars, costing from £52 to £59. Then there were two V-twins, the Orion and Libra with 5 hp and 8 hp engines. Grigg Motorcycles had become popular with sidecar owners, so these larger machines were usually sold complete with sidecars, as the 1923 Grigg advertisement shows *(fig 85)*. By 1923, a 1000 cc water-cooled

Grigg MOTOR CYCLES

on the most favourable

CASH or EASY PAYMENT TERMS

£72 - 10 - 0

3½ h.p COMBINATION, 3 speed Sturmey-Archer Gear, Clutch and Kick Starter, Dynamo Electric Lighting Set, Dunlop Tyres, ready for the road

Machines packed with two spare tyres, spare parts, etc., carriage paid for Export, £12 10s. extra.

Before deciding on your new machine, write for
1923 CATALOGUE
showing full range of models.

GRIGG LIMITED,

Winchester Works, Twickenham, S.W.

London Showrooms and Export Dept.
45, NEWMAN ST., W.1.

Fig 85

machine topped the range. Business was so good that plans were made to build a new, larger factory in South Croydon.

However, by the mid-1920s, the post-war boom was over and the Great Depression was on the horizon. Demand for motorcycles, like motorcars, was dropping dramatically and many companies were badly hit. Grigg became one of the casualties and by 1925 the factory had closed. The Winchester Works itself was demolished c1930 in the road clearance programme for the arterial Great Chertsey Road (A316) that cut a swathe through the streets of St Margarets (*see fig 83*).

At least three, possibly four, Grigg motorcycles have survived:

- ND 2939, an early Grigg scooter at the Hull Street Life Museum
- ND 4296, a 1923 343 cc Villiers engined motorcycle at the National Motorcycle Museum in Solihull
- BF 6928, a 1923 1000cc V-Twin with a Bacher and Hallon engine now at the Sammy Miller Museum, New Milton, Hants
- a 700 cc V-Twin of 1923 is believed to be in Ireland undergoing restoration.

Martinshaw Motorcycles

Martinshaw produced motorcycles in Twickenham between 1923 and 1925. They launched an ambitious range in 1923, all with Blackburne engines, from a 348cc single-cylinder model to a 998 cc V-Twin. The range had shrunk to two of the smaller models, the 348 cc and 545 cc, by 1924. Both had Sturmey-Archer gearboxes and chain drive. The two models continued to be produced during 1925 with Moss gearboxes. Production ceased later that year.

No Martinshaw motorcycles or photographs of them appear to have survived. The location of the Martinshaw works is unknown.

Wooler Engineering Co.

Fig 86

Wooler Engineering moved to Twickenham in 1925 to work in collaboration with Grigg's Motorcycles. John Wooler had designed and produced his first motorcycle in 1909 at his Harrow works. Output of the single-cylinder two-stroke motorcycle ceased between 1914 and 1918 as with most engineering firms. In 1919, the Wooler Mule cyclecar was announced in the 1919 advertisement *(fig 86)* for Wooler motorcycles. Production shifted first to Alperton and then to Twickenham in 1925. Here, Harry Grigg undertook production of John Wooler's designs for a while at the Winchester Works *(see fig 83)*. By 1930, Wooler Motorcycles had also disappeared.

Limited production of Wooler motor bikes restarted in 1945 but ceased again in 1956 when John Wooler died.

A number of Wooler motorcycles have survived, including:

- KE 3001, privately owned but on display at the National Motor Museum, Beaulieu
- WB 5397, sold by Bonham's for £13,800 in 2010.

Two different motorcycle makers used the Beaufort Works in East Twickenham during the 1920s - the same works where the Beaufort bus had been built (Chapter 5). WGC Hayward & Co. built aircraft parts there during the First World War and after refurbishing the works, turned their engineering skills to making motor scooters. The Argson company moved to Twickenham in 1922, taking over the Beaufort Works from WGC Hayward & Co. They built the light-weight Beaufort Motorcycle and a light motor tricycle designed as an invalid carriage, which shared the same 170cc engine as the motorcycle.

WGC Hayward & Co.

Fig 87

Haywards produced motor scooters in Twickenham between 1920 and 1921. Their scooter, the Whippet, was a neat little machine with a 150 cc two-stroke engine and a single speed. It had a flat platform and a bicycle saddle mounted above the engine. Like the motor scooter offered by Grigg Motorcycles at about the same time, it was aimed specifically at the aspiring 'lady' motorist, as the advertisement and cartoon confirm *(fig 87)*. There were three models including a *Sports* version, with a racing saddle and wide handlebars.

The company occupied the Beaufort Works where the Beaufort bus had previously been built *(refer to fig 42)*. However, demand for motor scooters was already declining and the business closed in 1921.

At least one Whippet has survived. The one seen in the photograph *(fig 88)* was restored by the Sammy Miller Museum for the British Motorcycle Charitable Trust.

Fig 88

Argson Engineering Co.

Argson (acronym of founders Arnold Ramsden Garnett and Stanley Orton Needham) first produced motor tricycles in 1920. The model was developed for those who had lost a limb in the First World War. The *'World's best tricycle'* as the advertisement claims *(fig 89)*. There was a large potential market for such a vehicle as many soldiers had been made invalid. The *'motor propelled'* model was powered by Argson's own 170 cc two-stroke engine, also used in their motorcycle. The company moved to Twickenham in 1922 when the Beaufort Works was vacated by WGC Hayward.

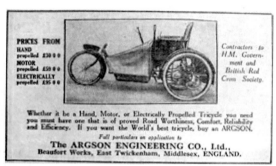

Fig 89

An electric powered version of the tricycle was added in 1923 and briefly a novel flat twin-cylinder 175 cc engined model in 1924. Electric powered transport had, of course, been pioneered in Twickenham over thirty years earlier on boats built on Eel Pie Island.

Argson invalid tricycles proved to be very popular with both private buyers and the British Government. The government took delivery of over two thousand machines for disabled servicemen. They continued in production until the 1930s.

After the Second World War, Argson invalid carriages were being built by the Stanley Engineering Co. Ltd. in Egham. Again, there was a large potential market of disabled ex-servicemen.

At least three Argson models have survived including:

- NPF 224, seen at classic car show in the photograph *(fig 90)*
- another is at Lakeland Motor Museum in Cumbria.

Fig 90

Another innovative motorcycle maker, Packham and Poppe (P&P), moved to Twickenham towards the end of the town's motorcycle manufacturing era. The works was located in Orleans Road, suggesting that it was the same premises at No.10 Orleans Road discussed in Chapter 3. However No.19 was also an engineering works by the 1920s, listed as the *'Service Engineering Co.'* in 1923.

There appears to be no connection between Austrian born Erling Poppe and German born Poppe brothers at the Poppe Rubber and Tyre Co. in Twickenham.

Packman & Poppe Ltd.

P&P built motorcycles in Orleans Road, Twickenham in 1925, moving later to Wembley. As well as the Twickenham and Wembley addresses, *The World's Motorcycles 1894-1963* lists two Coventry addresses for the

Fig 91

company. The photograph *(fig 91)* of an experimental Packman and Poppe two-stroke machine appeared in *The Motor Cycle,* 20th April 1922.

P&P made one of the first serious attempts to reduce engine noise while at the same time keeping the machine and rider clean by introducing the superbly silenced and fully enclosed Silent Three with 350 cc Barr & Stroud sleeve-valve power unit. Other models had JAP engines from 250 to1000 cc. Production of P&P machines continued with interruptions until 1930.

Erling Poppe went on to design motorcycles for Sunbeam, and the Gordon three-wheeler car. The Gordon was built by Vernons Industries Ltd, subsidiary of Vernon Pools, and was the cheapest motorcar on the British market in the 1950s.

Five P&P motorcycles are believed to have survived but only two are thought to remain in Europe:

- NU 2403, 1923 JAP 350 cc engine. Sold recently in original condition. Believed to be undergoing restoration in 2020.
- a 1927 Twin-port MAG engine in largely original condition.

F M Avey of Teddington

Avey was a motorcycle maker in Teddington, c1915. Engineer George Ward joined the company after working with John Carden who had, a year earlier, produced a cyclecar the Carden Monocar. Ward and Avey then went into business together as Ward and Avey Ltd. to produce the AV Monocar in Teddington, discussed in Chapter 8.

8. VEHICLES MADE IN TEDDINGTON, HAMPTON HILL AND HAMPTON

A LITTLE MORE THAN a mile south of Eel Pie Island, cars were being manufactured in Teddington, Hampton and Hampton Hill, part of the Borough of Twickenham from 1937.

The Carden Monocar and Ward & Avey Ltd.

Ward and Avey Ltd. in Somerset Road, Teddington bought the rights to build a cyclecar from John Carden. The wooden-bodied single-seat Monocar was initially built in Farnham, Surrey, before moving to larger premises in Teddington in February 1914. At its peak, Ward and Avey employed eighty people and produced one of the most popular of all the cyclecars. It also had the largest production run of any of the locally built cars: believed to have been a thousand cars, though not all were built in Teddington.

The photograph *(fig 92)* shows John Carden at the wheel of a 1914 model.

Fig 92

Fig 93

The Carden Monocar was advertised *(fig 93)* in 1916 at the Somerset Road, Teddington address. The photograph *(fig 94)* shows a Monocar being manually lowered from the upper floor of the premises in Somerset Road, Teddington. It appears that the works was a former stables. The buildings may earlier have been associated with Astley Lodge, a large house in Church Road.

Carden's cycle car was powered by a 481 cc JAP single-cylinder engine driving the back wheels via a belt. It had no gearbox and it was not thought necessary to have a differential as the thirty-inch track was so narrow.

The company, its assets and the design were sold to George Ward in 1916. By 1918, he and Frederick Avey (the motorcycle maker mentioned in Chapter 7) had established Ward and Avey Ltd. who renamed the car the AV Monocar and continued to build it at the Somerset Road works. AV offered a JAP, Blackburne or MAG engine, a two-speed or three-

Fig 94

speed Sturmey-Archer gearbox and chain drive. The car bodies were not made at the factory but by the Thames Valley Pattern Works in nearby Elmtree Road. The bodywork was made of plywood, mahogany or even compressed paper, to keep the weight down to a mere 250 kg. The Monocar was described humorously in *The Motor Cycle* magazine as *'a low coffin shaped projectile, moderately attractive in dense fog'!* [31]. The map *(fig 95)* shows the location of the Somerset Road works, close to the junction with Church Road.

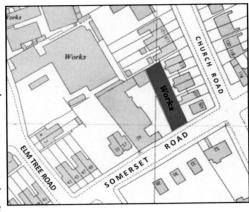

Fig 95

By 1919, the Bi-car had been launched, with the passenger sitting tandem style behind the driver and the car's width increased to 36 inches.

The advertisement (fig 96) offers 'Efficiency, combined with economy' from the AV two-seater. A side-by-side model, the Runabout, was added in 1921. The Monocar and Bi-car were both dropped in 1922, leaving only the Runabout in production. The company was renamed AV Motors in 1923 but ceased manufacturing motorcars the following year. The company had already moved to Park Road, Teddington, and remained in business for many years as a Jowett, and later, a Rootes Group dealership. John Carden also sold the rights to manufacture a two-seater Bi-car to Tamplin Engineering Company in November 1919. Tamplin Cyclecars were manufactured in Kingston Road, Staines until 1923 and from 1924 to 1925 in Malden Road, Cheam (see Chapter 9).

Carden designed a further version in 1922 and sold the rights to build it to Arnott and

A car which looks right and is right, either for business or pleasure.

The "A.V." Two-Seater

Efficiency, combined with economy.

Reprinted Specification with fuller information now available.

WARD & AVEY, LTD.,

Registered Offices and Works:

Somerset Road, Teddington.

Fig 96

Harrison of Hythe Road, Willesden. This version of the cyclecar was sold as the New Carden and continued in production until 1925.

Fig 97 (above)

Fig 98 (below)

The photograph *(fig 97)* shows the Church Road side of the site while the Monocar was in production. The second photograph *(fig 98)* shows the back wall of the building on the right of the first photo, all that remains of the works today.

A remarkable number of these small cars have survived.

Carden Monocars of the original type:
- NH 3610 owned by Gerry Michelmore, seen in the photograph *(fig 99)*
- NY 87 which was part of the A.W.F. Smith collection is now also in regular use.
- A third Carden Monocar is also believed to have survived.

AV Monocars:
- UB 5357 belonging to Mike Bullett of the VSCC and is in regular use.
- Possibly one more.

New Carden Monocars:
- PE 6048 owned by Mark Longmore, PD 3235 & XR 9586.

Tamplin Monocars:
- BL 8547, BW 3779, Y 7731 and MD 7280, a very smart example in the Louwman Museum in Belgium.

The AV Monocar illustrates the blurred lines that divided motorcars and motor cycles in the early part of the twentieth century. It could be said that the Monocar was little more than a motorcycle masquerading as a car by the addition of a flimsy body and two bicycle-style wheels. It is also typical of the most successful locally made cars, aimed at those aspiring to be car owners who couldn't afford the cost of a 'real' motorcar. This had become a huge market that the Austin 7

Fig 99

exploited when it went into production in 1923, using the economies of mass production. In turn, this spelled the end of the road for the small hand-made motor manufacturers like those in the Twickenham area.

Teddington also hosted two motor engineering companies on the banks of the River Thames. They were on adjacent sites on the same riverside industrial area bordered by Manor Road, Twickenham Road and the river. Teddington Motorcar and Launch Works built motorboats and is believed to have been involved in manufacturing motor car and aeroplane engines. This mirrors what was happening at engineering works in Twickenham, a mile downstream. The other, Monarch Motor Co., built motorboats and is thought to have entered the cycle car market between 1925 and 1928. Monarch's motor works had earlier been used by the Franco-Belgian engineer Charles Pelabon. In October 1914, Pelabon started to produce munitions in the disused works. His workers were Belgian refugees who had fled from the German army. Pelabon moved to a larger factory in East Twickenham which later housed the Berliet motor company (Chapter 6).

The Pelabon works turned to producing motorcar parts after the First World War.

Teddington Motorcar and Launch Works

John Hesse and Gerald Savory set up a manufacturing partnership to make motorboats and cars in Twickenham Road, Teddington in 1905. The site and works can be seen on the Goad map of 1907 shown earlier *(see fig 45)*. By 1909 they were manufacturing gearboxes for boats. A key selling point for their boats was the Hesse Patented Reversing Gear, reviewed in *Engineering* magazine on 26th March 1909.

The business had around forty employees. Robert Bamford joined the partnership which continued until at least 1913. Soon after, they went their own ways, Hesse joining Thornycroft and Bamford joining Lionel

Fig 100

Martin to form Bamford and Martin. By 1926 Bamford and Martin had become the iconic Aston Martin Motors with their famous logo *(fig 100)*. Aston Martin was based nearby in Feltham.

Monarch Motor Co. Ltd.

From 1901, Monarch Motor Launches were operating from a boathouse on the river near Manor Road. The boathouse was adjacent to the area

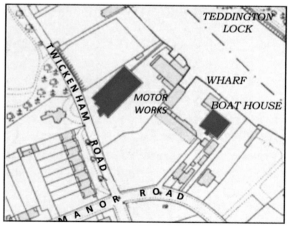

Fig 101

marked *'Wharf'* on the map *(fig 101)*. Principally they built motor launches like the one shown in the photograph *(fig 102)*. Monarch is also believed to have entered the cyclecar market between 1925 and 1928. Ward and Avey had been building the AV Monocar a cyclecar nearby, in Somerset Road,

Teddington until 1924. It would seem possible that Monarch based their car on an AV model. Production of the AV Tandem had already moved to Staines. How many cycle cars were made by Monarch is unknown - possibly only a prototype. However Monarch is listed as a motor manufacturer in Grace's Guide to British Industrial History.

Fig 102

Tough Brothers Boatbuilders bought the site in the 1920s. The Monarch boathouse and workshop, shown in the photograph *(fig 103a)*, became their main office. The building has survived and is now The Wharf restaurant *(fig 103b)*. The photographs of the Wharf taken in March 2020 *(figs 104a & b)* shows the building virtually unchanged on the southern and eastern sides except for the addition of a sympathetically designed kitchen block. The boathouse on the northern side of the works has been demolished and the river facing side largely obscured by an enclosed verandah. The main works/ boathouse is nevertheless still clearly recognisable.

Figs 103a and 103b (top)

Figs 104a and 104b (bottom)

Motor manufacturing resumed in the Borough of Twickenham in 1938 when the British Anzani company moved into premises in Windmill Road, Hampton Hill. The Italian Alessandro Anzani originally manufactured engines in France. The Anzani company produced engines for aircraft, cars, boats and motorcycles at factories in France, Italy and Britain.

AC cars followed when they took over the lease on Tagg's Island, Hampton in 1941. AC had been making cars just over the river in Thames Ditton since 1925. British Anzani appears to be the only motor manufacturer to have been based in Hampton Hill and AC the only one in Hampton.

British Anzani Engineering Co.

In 1912 the company was first established in London as the British Anzani Engine Co. They went on to supply engines to AC cars, including the 1,496 cc side-valve four-cylinder engine that would become their famous two-litre motor. They supplied Frazer-Nash with a 1,496 cc ohv engine, and Morgan with a V-twin, amongst others. Anzani also supplied engines for British motorcycles but their best-known products came to be lawnmowers and outboard motors.

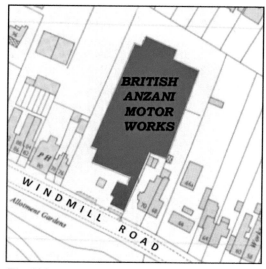

The company had been slowly failing during the 1930s. In 1938 Charles Henry Harrison, an ex-JAP apprentice and keen motorcycle and powerboat racer, took over as Chief Designer and Managing Director. He moved the company to Windmill Road in Hampton Hill shown on the map *(fig 105)*. The company became British Anzani Engineering Co. The

Fig 105

Fig 106

photograph *(fig 106)* shows the entrance to the works, which was quite close to The Windmill public house. In 1941 a planning application was submitted and approved to extend the works.

Fig 107

In 1940, British Anzani responded to the need for additional war-time food production with the innovative and the extremely successful Iron Horse two-wheeled tractor, shown in the advertisement *(fig 107)* and photograph *(fig 108)*. These popular machines proved robust and reliable and sold all around the world. They cost £140 in 1940 or could be bought on hire-purchase or even rented from the factory for £3.10s.0d. a week!

Fig 108

Fig 109

Fig 110

Production of agricultural tractors stopped in 1956. By then, Anzani were producing a range of outboard motors as the advertisement *(fig 109)*, shows as well as the Easimow and Easicut petrol-engined lawn mowers.

Grace's Guide also describes British Anzani as a *'small manufacturer of cars in the 1950s powered by the British Anzani engine'*. In the austerity years after the Second World War, Anzani produced a light car named the Astra Utility. It was marketed as *'ideal for tradesmen's deliveries, travellers, service engineers, etc'*, as the advertisement shows *(fig 110)*. It had originally been developed by JARC Motors in Isleworth and known as the Little Horse. British Anzani installed their own 322 cc motorcycle engine into the rear underfloor engine compartment and changed some design specifications.

With a steel chassis and a lightweight aluminium body supported on a pine frame, a load carrying capacity of 3.5 cwt, a 15 bhp engine and the three speed gearbox gave a top speed of 55 mph, and 60 mpg. It seated two in relative comfort at an on-the-road price of £347.16s.0d including purchase tax. The Astra claimed to be the smallest and cheapest four-wheeler on the British market *(fig 111)*. It was in production from 1956 until 1959. Although not a huge sales success, it was very much in the same 'light car' tradition as Twickenham motorcars from a generation or two earlier.

Fig 111

After Anzani ceased production, some coupés of the Astra design were made by Gill cars and sold as the Getabout. The rights were also bought by Harold Lightburn in Adelaide, Australia who fitted a new glass-fibre estate body and sold the car as the Zeta between 1963 and 1966.

The British Anzani Group finally went into liquidation in 1980. The factory was demolished and the Sanders Close housing development built on the site.

At least two Astras are known to have survived:

- 566 CPC: Green, 1956. This car was housed at the Kew Motor Museum until 1999. It was sold by Brightwell's Classic Car Auctions for £2800. Present whereabouts unknown.
- 192 XUM: Green, 1956. Now at the Lane Motor Museum in Nashville, Tennessee, USA. Shown in the photographs *(figs 112 a/b/c)*. It is part of a collection of unusual European cars. The photographs overleaf show the rather basic nature of the Astra Utility.

British Anzani continued in the Twickenham light car tradition, producing vehicles aimed at those who might otherwise not have been able to afford motorised transport. Interestingly, there is *Pathe News* footage of the launch of *'a new British car, the British Anzani Astra'* - one of the few pieces of contemporary film of a Twickenham built car.

Figs 112a, 112b and 112c

AC similarly started with a light delivery vehicle, a three-wheeler, before moving into light car production. AC went on to become a specialist sports car maker in Thames Ditton. At the Tagg's Island site in the Borough of Twickenham, AC returned to building three-wheeler cars after the Second World War, this time as invalid cars.

AC Cars at Tagg's Island, Hampton

AC Cars (originally Autocarriers Ltd) was established at the turn of the century in West Norwood by John Weller and John Portwine. At first they built a small three-wheeler delivery vehicle, known as The Auto-Carrier. In 1907, a passenger version was launched, called the Tricar. In October 1911, they moved the business to a larger factory in Thames Ditton, as the 1912 advertisement shows *(fig 113)*, the Tricar now apparently renamed the AC Sociable. By 1913, AC had developed its first four-wheel vehicle, the AC Light Car. AC turned to the British Anzani company, later located in Hampton Hill, for a new larger engine. They selected a 1500 cc, 11.8 hp four-cylinder engine which was made by AC from 1925 in their Thames Ditton factory. It was used to power almost every AC model from 1922 until 1963, with its power output gradually increasing from 40 to 105 bhp.

During the Second World War the company started manufacturing guns, flame throwers, firefighting equipment, radar vans and aircraft parts for the Fairey Aircraft Company. Demand for this military work was such that in 1941, William Hurlock, AC's managing director, bought the lease of Tagg's Island. The island hotel, which had formerly been Fred Karno's 'Karsino', and its

Fig 113

extensive grounds were taken over. The skating rink and tennis courts provided the site for the factory. The aerial photograph *(fig 114)* shows Taggs Island, the hotel and tennis courts before the bridge was built to connect the Island to the Hampton mainland.

Fig 114

91

After the war the company switched once again to building three-wheelers, this time, 'invalid cars' for injured ex-servicemen returning from fighting in the Second World War *(fig 115)*. Known as the Model 70 or AC

Fig 115

70, it was purpose built for the Ministry of Pensions. Launched in 1947, it was developed over the next 20 years to have a 500 cc flat-twin which could reach a top speed of 55 mph.

Other AC products made at the Tagg's Island factory included four seven-carriage trains *(fig 116)* for the 1.34 mile long pier at Southend-on-sea in 1949. Three of these AC carriages are preserved at the Southend Pier museum. Somewhat bizarrely, AC diversified in the early 1950s, making the "Bag Boy" folding golf trolley under US licence.

ONE OF THE FOUR NEW ELECTRIC TRAINS - SOUTHEND PIER

Fig 116

Production of AC's invalid carriages ceased on Tagg's Island in the mid-1960s and the factory closed soon after. Production was transferred to their Thames Ditton factory where AC sports cars had been made throughout the 1950s. AC's range included the Ace, Aceca and Greyhound and in 1962, the legendary AC Cobra.

The Thames Ditton factory finally closed in 1984.

A few of the many AC 70s built appear to have survived despite becoming illegal to drive on British roads in 2003.

- GPG 721K is at the Riverside Museum in Glasgow
- RRF19R is at the Lakeland Motor Museum *(fig 117)*

Fig 117

9. LOCAL MOTORING FAMILY BUSINESSES

THE STORY OF Twickenham's Motorcars would not be complete without reference to the pioneering motoring family businesses that, although not manufacturers, were nonetheless part of the story and deserve mention. All started as bicycle makers at the turn of the 20th century, the dawn of motoring. Tamplin's and Kingsbury's were local family businesses synonymous with motorcars, Blay's and Palmer's with motorcycling. Kingsbury's in Hampton is the only one of these pioneering family ventures to still be in business today (2024).

Other local garages have long and interesting histories, like Orleans Garage, mentioned in Chapter 4 and Mercury Motors in Strawberry Vale, with a particularly interesting and unusual story.

Although the importance of coach builders to the emergence of the local motor industry has already been made clear, only Corben's role has been explored so far (Chapter 6). Coach building, in particular of commercial vehicles, continued in Twickenham after much of the motor industry had disappeared, as did the motor component industry. Both were usually family businesses and deserve a little more attention.

Tamplin's of Twickenham

William Frederick Tamplin was a cycle maker in Twickenham in the late 19th and early 20th century. His connection with the Orleans cars was explored in Chapter 3.

WF Tamplin was in business as a cycle maker at No.4 Staines Road Terrace, Twickenham Green from c1900. The photograph shows Tamplin outside the shop. The photograph must have been taken after the King Street and Heath Road premises had been acquired, as both are mentioned on the signboard *(fig 118)* and his business card *(fig 118a)*. WF Tamplin continued to run the cycle business from this site until 1919. It had been renumbered 38 The Green, Twickenham by 1910. It then became Tamplin Automobile Specialists and continued at this address until 1927. An advertisement from the period *(fig 119)* shows a photograph of the shop and the cycle works, clearly the first floor of 12, King Street. It would appear that Tamplin continued to make the *'Orleans'* cycle taking it over from Henry Burford. Interestingly, Tamplin described his business as *'Cycle and Motor Manufacturers'*. Frank Obey was Tamplin's manager. The photograph *(fig 120)* shows the King Street premises of *'W.F. Tamplin'*, offering, *'Motor & Cycle repairs'* at street level. John Ellis Thurlston, apprentice to Tamplin, can be seen standing in the doorway. The first floor housed the cycle works. By 1908, WF Tamplin was still at No.12 King Street site, although the Orleans Cycle Company was no longer trading from there.

Fig 118

William's son, Edward Alfred Tamplin, was described in the 1911 census as a motor mechanic. He established Tamplin Engineering

Fig 118a

Fig 119

Fig 120

Co. which, in 1919, acquired the rights to build the 4-wheeled cyclecar originally designed by Sir John Carden and later manufactured by Ward and Avey in Teddington (Chapter 8). The popular Tamplin cyclecar was produced between 1919 and 1923. A larger side-by-side model was produced in 1924/5. Tamplin did not build the car in Twickenham but in Kingston Road, Staines, and later in Malden Road, Cheam.

Tamplin's Motor Co. was incorporated in June 1921 and Tamplin's Garage was opened in Heath Road Twickenham, *(see fig 31).* Tamplin's

Fig 121a   *Fig 121b opposite*

showroom was at No.12 King Street on the corner with Cross Deep *(figs 121a/b)* on the right of the photograph behind the signpost. Tamplin was selling Wolseley cars, amongst others, from the showroom at their King Street site, as the signboard in the photograph shows. The premises had earlier been leased by Burford and Van Toll (Chapter 3). The map *(fig 122)* shows the impact on the Tamplin site (shaded) and Pound Lane behind, of widening King Street.

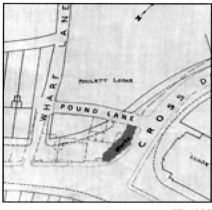

Fig 122

After King Street was widened in 1929, Tamplin's opened a prestigious car showroom at No.66 York Street on the corner with Church Street in Twickenham, seen in the photograph *(fig 123)*, trading as Tamplin & Pangbourne. Tamplin's Servicing and Repairs depot was sited initially in Holly Road and later opposite Old Station Yard at No.2 Queens Road, seen on the far right the photograph *(figs 124a/b)*. Tamplin's was established at this site from the 1920s until the latter part of the 20th century. By the 1990s the workshop was being used by *'Refurb-a-Sash'* and had become a gym by 2021 when the photograph *(fig 125)* was taken.

Fig 123

Fig 124a

Fig 124b   *Fig 125*

Tamplin's Garage moved back to Heath Road in Twickenham to the site previously occupied by Spikins of Twickenham.

Tamplin Cycle Cars that are known to have survived:

- MD 7280 (1921) now in the Louwman Museum, in the Netherlands.
- BL 8547 (1921) owned by Peter Harper (1995).
- Y 7731 (1921) owned by Alan Whitehead (1995).
- 3779 Thought to be experimental 1918 works car, owned by Chris Gordon (1995). [32]

Kingsbury's of Hampton

Kingsbury's of Hampton deserves particular mention as it has been in business for over 120 years, spanning the entire history of the motorcar. The firm was founded in 1897, initially as a bicycle maker and repairer, the year that the first car was manufactured in Britain. A few years later, Kingsbury's became one of the earliest motor traders in the Twickenham area. Kingsbury's are still trading in Station Road Hampton as motor agents, offering car sales and repairs today (2024).

The firm started as George Kingsbury and Son. Cycle Manufacturers, making and repairing bicycles at 3, Red Lion Square, Hampton seen in the 1908 photograph *(fig 126)*. Their earliest reference as a motor trader, was the sale of a motorcycle in December 1904. It was a Royal Enfield 2 ¾ hp Minerva, sold for £25 0s 0d to a Mr Phelps, who had a well-known local furniture business. Kingsbury's had moved into the motoring era. There is no evidence that Kingsbury produced their own motor-cycles, despite early involvement with motorcycles and as bicycle makers.

Fig 126

In 1906, Mr Phelps purchased a two-seater motorcar from Kingsbury's for £175. Kingsbury's had now entered the business of selling cars. George Kingsbury had bought his

Fig 127

own first car, a Humber 10/12, in 1905, shown in the photograph *(fig 127)*. He may well have been the first person to own a car in Hampton. Today (2024), Nick Kingsbury is the fourth generation of Kingsbury's to be involved in the family business with the company's 125th anniversary held in 2022.

CA Blay at Twickenham Green

A very familiar name to motorcyclists and Twickenham residents alike for many decades was CA Blay or 'Blay's', with their bright red-painted shopfronts and premises dotted around the Twickenham Green area until the mid 2000s. The sight and sound of motorbikes was never far away.

Fig 128

Charles Albert Blay opened his first premises, at No.2 Briar Road just off the Green in c1912. The photograph *(fig 128)* shows the premises, which advertised cycle making and *'Motor Cycle Repair Specialists'*. By 1915, CA Blay had opened at a second location, No.192 Twickenham Green. By 1928, Blay had taken over WF Tamplin's premises at No.38, Twickenham Green, formerly known as 4 Staines Road Terrace. Blay's later went on to acquire the three adjoining properties, Nos 32-36. Tamplin moved into the King Street premises that he already owned, previously leased to the Orleans Cycle Company.

The photograph *(fig 129)* taken c1930, shows CA Blay's premises at 192, Heath Road with Charles Blay, his daughter Anne and Jim Gilkes, whom she later married. The motorcycle in the picture is a 'Trusty' Triumph Model 'P' from c1915.

Blay's went on to acquire a number of premises dotted around the Green each of which had different specialisms: bicycle sales and repairs, motorcycle sales, repairs and spare parts. Blay's also starting selling cars in the 1930s, or certainly three-wheelers, like the revolutionary front-wheel-drive BSA seen in the advertisement *(fig 130)*.

Fig 129

Nos 32-36 Twickenham Green became the hub of their motorcycle business. 192, Heath Road became the motorcycle spares shop, and 197 opposite, was the repairs workshop. By 1920, No.18 Staines Road was Blay's cycle shop, run by Joe Vine, Charles Blay's nephew.

Fig 130

Charles Blay's son Ken took over the reins of the family business when 'Charlie' retired. Not surprisingly, Ken was a motorcycle enthusiast, seen in the photograph *(fig 131)* *'always out riding, scrambling, stunt riding at Hanworth Park,*

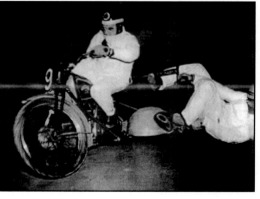

Fig 131

sidecar racing with his wife Molly, grass-track racing and playing motorcycle football' [33]. Molly ran the business with Ken for many years and throughout the Second World War.

The end of Blay's and their contribution to Twickenham's motoring history began when the Blay family sold the business to Paul Buffery in 2006. Initially, Blay's continued to run much as before but Buffery had ambitions to capitalise on the development potential of the company's premises. The buildings at 32-38 Twickenham Green were sold off in 2006. This is now a *'Sainsbury's Local'* supermarket. No.192 Heath Road had already burnt to the ground after petrol was reportedly poured through the letterbox, in the aftermath of the Tottenham riots. It didn't reopen. The final premises from which Blay's traded was 199 Heath Road, used as the workshop until 2006 and then the spares department until it too finally closed.

Bob Anderson, who provided much of the information for this section, worked for Blay's for 52 years and was managing director from 1974 until the company finally closed their last shop in 2008.

Palmer's of Teddington

Fig 132

Palmer's Cycle Stores was opened by Charles James Palmer in Stanley Road, Teddington c1904. The shop, No.8 King's Parade, was newly built and became No.81 Stanley Road, later renumbered No.109. James Palmer hand-built *'Palmer's Cycles'* from the frame upwards. The photograph *(fig 132)* shows James outside the shop, with a range of his bikes, including a tandem and a

Fig 133

wicker bath chair which could be attached to a bicycle, a forerunner of today's child-transporter trailers. The picture of the Mid-Surrey Cycling Club, *(fig 133)* hung in the shop. James is in the third row directly above the rear wheel of the three-seater bicycle, presumably a Palmer's Cycle built by James. His family lived over the shop and son Aubrey Edward Palmer later took over the running of the business. Aubrey was a keen motorcyclist and member of the *'Twickenham & District Motor Cycle Club'*, like Ken Blay mentioned above. In common with other bicycle shops, Palmer's developed their business between the two world wars to include motor vehicles. Petrol was also sold from petrol pumps on the pavement, seen in the photograph *(fig 134)*.

By 1955, when Palmer's became a limited company, Aubrey's son David had joined the business. Palmer's offered a full range of services for the vehicles they sold including spares,

Fig 134

Fig 135

repairs and, later, MOTs. In the 1950s and 60s, motorcycles, motor scooters and the Trojan three-wheeler bubble-cars were sold. Palmer's had expanded by then, adding showrooms at Nos 119 and 121, a few doors away from No.109 *(fig 135)*. The photograph shows scooters and a bubble car for sale, with Geoff Grace the spares manager outside No.119 and Joy and David Palmer visible inside No.121. Palmer's was an agent and distributor for Lambretta *(fig 136)* and a number of motorcycle brands, including Greeves and Suzuki. Palmer's was a honey pot for *'Mods'* in the 1960s, to buy their Lambretta scooters and accessories. By the 1970s, the Yamaha FS1E light motorcycle had become the teenagers 'must have' moped. Later, David Palmer concentrated on the rise in popularity of mountain bikes.

Fig 136

David Palmer shared his father Aubrey's enthusiasm for off-road motorcycling sports like scrambling and grass-track racing. The photograph shows David Palmer outside the showroom in Stanley Road with his grass-track bike with a Greeves Griffon engine *(fig 137)*. Dave Palmer, as he was known when he raced, was *'Works rider'* for the highly successful Greeves Motorcycle company. Greeves was regularly winning competitions before Suzuki started to dominate European championships in the 1970s.

Palmer's remained in business for many years in Stanley Road selling and repairing bicycles once again. When David Palmer retired at the age of 81 in 2015, Palmer's was the oldest family run business in Teddington. His wife Joy and daughter, Claire Palmer, provided much of the information and photographs for this section.

Fig 137

There was also a 'Palmer's Cycle Store' at 53 York Street in Twickenham, which may have been run by another member of the family. The family believe he may have been an uncle.

In the first half of the twentieth century, garages or motor engineering companies as they were usually known, would provide all the necessary services for the motorist. They would sell petrol, initially served from petrol cans, before petrol pumps became a common feature. Engine oil was decanted from oil drums into a pint or quart jug before being poured into the engine. Servicing and repairs were also a major part of their work, usually requiring engineering skills to remake broken or worn parts. In a few cases, motorcars were manufactured on the same premises, as already mentioned, at motor engineering companies in the Twickenham area.

Mercury Motors: motor engineering – not just a 'job for the boys'

The story of Mercury Motors started with two young women, Meg Caley and Molly Sweet. In 1936 Meg worked at a garage in Hounslow. She became friendly with Molly at a drama club in Twickenham. Molly's mother died and left her some money, so in 1941 she set up Mercury Engineering Co. in Twickenham *(fig 138)*.

Fig 138

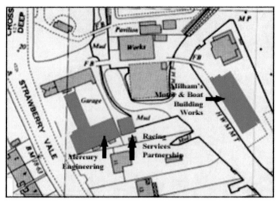

Fig 139

Molly Sweet rented 5-7 Strawberry Vale *(see fig 139)* and chose the company name after her favourite metal, mercury. Initially, much of the engineering work was making parts for the war effort, including the making and fitting of gas-bag roof frames to cars (as seen in *fig 141* below).

Unexpectedly, Molly was called up for war service, so she asked her friend Meg to stand in for her at Mercury. The business was going through hard times but Meg struggled on, at one point without pay. By 1944 the business was doing much better and Molly bought the freehold of the site. Ted Budd, Meg's brother-in-law started to work at Mercury and Meg married Brian Rees.

However in 1948, Molly decided to emigrate to New Zealand. Meg couldn't afford to buy the freehold from Molly, but was granted a lease by the new freeholder - at double the rent! During the 1950s Meg ran the motoring side of the business on her own.

Petrol was already sold on the site before it became Mercury Engineering Co., as the photograph taken in 1929 shows *(fig 140)*. The photograph *(fig 141)* taken in war-time 1940s, shows a car with white painted mudguards, black-out headlamps and gas bag on the car roof. Town gas was used in place of petrol as petrol was in very short supply. It also shows the new sign above the workshop doors stating *'Production*

Fig 140

Fig 141

Automobile and Marine Engineers'. It is unclear what marine engineering Mercury undertook.

By the 1950s, Mercury Motors was thriving. A car showroom and spares department were added to the servicing and repairs workshop already on the site, as the photograph *(fig 142)* shows. In 1956 Mercury became a Ford retail dealer, selling new cars, car spares, servicing and repairs, as well as selling petrol. In 1963 Meg and Brian bought the freehold of the garage site for £25,000. In the late 1960s, Meg's two sons

Fig 142

Fig 143

Anthony and Robin joined the business. Anthony soon took over the running of the workshop and Robin the spares department. Ted ran the petrol sales. Meg remained in overall charge of the garage.

Meg never formally retired, though the running of Mercury Motors was left to her two sons, Anthony and Robin, who provided the information and photographs for this section. The business is still run by Robin and Anthony's son, Simon (2024). The petrol pumps now lie idle, stored at the back of the workshop. The photograph *(fig 143)* shows the first Mercury Motors pick-up truck, a Ford E83W. Anthony wishes they'd kept it. Simon Rees is the third generation of the family to be involved in the business, as his grandmother Meg had hoped. Mercury Motors remains one of the few family run garages still offering a range of motoring services in Twickenham.

***

Local coach builders were a key reason for the development of Twickenham's motor industry. There were a number of coach builders in Heath Road: Corben's at the junction with Cross Deep, Mrs Giles & Son at No.26, Walter Biggs on the site that later became Obey's Garage and G&T Gravestock nearby at No.4 The Green.

Coach builders turned their skills to car body making but as car making declined, they became involved in commercial vehicle body building. The St Margaret's area of East Twickenham also had a long history of involvement with coach building, starting with Elijah Thornton in the early 1900s. In Teddington commercial vehicle body building would appear to have started later but also continued later into the 20th century.

The making of motor vehicle components also continued in Twickenham into the latter part of the 20th century. The Poppe Rubber and Tyre company moved into the former Orleans car factory (see Chapter 3) in Sherland Road in 1932 and produced motorcar tyres and rubber components for the motor and aircraft industries.

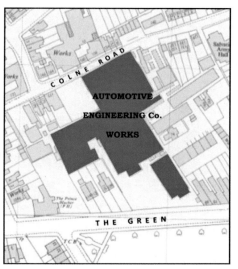

Fig 144

Manufacturing had stopped at the site by 1985 and Twickenham's first car factory was demolished a year or so later.

There were other motor parts and components manufacturers but the Automotive Engineering Company, established in 1929, was probably the largest. The engineering works was on a substantial site between Twickenham Green and Colne Road, as the 1936 map shows *(fig 144)*. The company was best known for making pistons for car engines, like the BHB self-adjusting pistons shown in the

Fig 145

advertisement *(fig 145)*. BHB stood for Bentley, Hewitt and Burgess and according to the book *Bentley Factory Cars 1919 - 1931… '80% of the cars parts were made by Automotive Engineering Co, Twickenham'* [34]. BHB also cooperated in the design of pistons which were used in both Rolls Royce cars and aero engines which according to Spencer Silverbach, *'may have saved thousands of airmen because of the BHB piston'* [34]. By 1936 they had 535 employees [8]. The factory closed c1990.

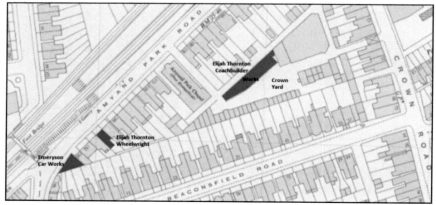

Fig 146

Elijah Thornton and Arlington Works

Elijah Thornton established a wheelwrights at 156, Amyand Park Road in c1903. By 1905, he was described as a *'coach builder'* at the same address [35]. In 1919, he was a 'Coach and Carriage Builder' a couple of hundred yards away. By 1920 Elijah Thornton was listed in the *London City Directory* as a *'Motor Builder'* at Crown Yard. It would seem likely that he would have been building the bodywork for one of the local motor manufacturing companies. The map *(fig 146)* shows these two locations and also the location of the Emeryson motor works in Amyand Park Road, some years later (Chapter 10). Interestingly Crown Yard still has motoring connections today (2024). Crown Classic Cars Ltd has been established there for many years, repairing and restoring classic cars, particularly sports cars.

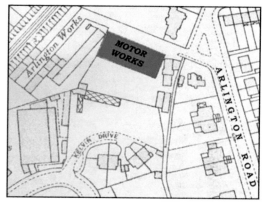

There was also a *'Motor Works'* in Arlington Road, St Margarets adjacent to Arlington Works, shown on the 1935 map *(fig 147)*. The photograph *(fig 148)* shows that the Wilson Motor Body Building Co. established at the site, offering *'A Body For*

Fig 147

Fig 148

Every Trade' at the time that the aerial photograph was taken in the 1930s. Presumably they were coach building commercial vehicle bodies on to chassis built locally. Joseph Chirm Wilson and *Wilson Body Building Co.* are registered at the Arlington Works from c1928 [36]. At the time of the 1911 census, Joseph was a cycle

Fig 149

maker in Battersea. He was born in Birmingham but moved to Coventry. By 1911 his son, Sidney James Wilson, was aged 18 and also a cycle maker.

The large building, to the far left of the photograph would appear to be the *Motor Works* marked on the 1935 map. Whether the *'Motor Works'* was part of Wilson's has not been possible to ascertain. The long corrugated-iron-clad structure with Wilson's advertising slogan on the roof, was still in use at the time of the May 2020 photograph *(fig 149)*. Whether this formed part of the motor works is unclear. One part of the site retained a motoring connection until at least 2020, housing Arlington Auto Precision. The site of the building marked *'Motor Works'* on the map, has since been replaced by flats.

Interestingly, one 'car', a baby carriage or pram - the Harford Baby Car - was being manufactured at the Arlington Works in the 1920s, as the advertisement in the Daily Mirror shows *(fig 150)*.

Fig 150

P & S Motors Ltd, and Palmer Coachbuilder Ltd, Teddington

Fig 151

Commercial vehicle bodies were built at No.99 Waldegrave Road in Teddington in the mid 20th century. The company listed in *Burt's Directory* for 1953 is *'P & S Motors Ltd, Automobile Engineers & Body Builders'*. Earlier, petrol was also sold at the site, as the photograph shows *(fig 151)*. The film *Virginia* advertised on one of the posters in the photograph was released in 1941, so it would appear that in the 1940s, P & S Motors was selling and servicing Bedford commercial vehicles

Fig 153

as well as building bodies for them.

By the 1960s, Palmer Coachbuilder was at the site. The photographs *(figs 152)* taken by the author in 1964, show a fire that broke out in the engine compartment of one of the chassis awaiting body building, outside the works. The fire was quickly extinguished once the local fire brigade arrived.

An advertisement for Palmer in *The Commercial Motor* in April 1965, suggests that that they had moved to *'Western Works, Twickenham Road, Hanworth'* by then, still within the borough of Twickenham *(fig 153)*. There is apparently no connection between Palmer Coachbuilder and Palmer's of Teddington.

Figs 152

10. A Motoring Renaissance:

Twickenham's racing cars

URING THE SECOND half of the 20th century, Twickenham hosted a number of specialist racing car constructors. One continued into the 21st century. All were started by motor racing drivers and enthusiasts. Paul Emery built his cars to finance his own driving career, whilst Bob Spikin and John Willment used their racing to advertise the garages they had opened to fuel their motoring passions. The cars were very much in the Twickenham motorcars tradition, inexpensive but punching above their weight. The Costin-Nathan car is a good example of this and with its Eel Pie Island connection neatly brings Twickenham's motoring story back to where it had all started.

Emeryson Cars Ltd.

In the 1930s, George Emery started constructing racing *'specials'*. By the 1950s, his son Paul was constructing and driving Emeryson racing cars, based in Twickenham. In the early days Paul and his wife Barbara made up the racing team. Barbara *'helps him in the garage and acts as mechanic in competitions'* [33] according to a 1950 newspaper article. She also became a racing driver. The photograph *(fig 154)* shows Paul Emery in No.28, overtaking Jack Leary in No.21, a Cooper-Norton on a bend at Brands Hatch on 8th April 1951. Incidentally, Bernie Ecclestone gained 4th place in the final of the same race. As the Emeryson specification sheet *(fig 155)* shows, the car was priced at £650, very reasonable for a Formula 3 racing car. However this price did not include one of the choice of engines or gearboxes. Emeryson attracted some motor racing legends of the day like Colin Chapman to drive the cars. Paul Emery was described as a

Fig 154

```
Manufacturer:  Emeryson Cars.                          EMERYSON
Name of car:  Emeryson.
Price:  £650 less engine and gearbox.
Chassis
Type of frame:  Tubular (ladder type).
Material:  2¼in. x 16g. steel.
Disposition of frame members:  Straight tubes with four cross members.
Engine mounting:  ¼in. Dural plate.
Gearbox mounting:  Integral with engine plates.
Transmission:  Chain.
Engine cooling:  Air ducts.
Axle mounting (front and rear):  Tube torque box (incorporating suspension
     mounting).
Brakes:  Lockheed 2L-S.  Front 8in. x 1¼in., rear 8in. x 1¼in.
Steering mechanism:  Rack and pinion.
Suspension:  Front, wishbone with rubber or coil springs; rear, De Dion with
     rubber or coil springs.
Wheels:  Dunlop 15in.
Tyres:  Dunlop; 400 x 15 front, 450 x 15 rear.
Shock absorbers (front and rear):  Newton.
Body material:  Aluminium, detachable by Dzus fasteners (whole body).
Proprietary components used on car:  Smiths r.p.m. indicator; Lockheed brakes;
     Dunlop wheels and tyres; Newton shock-absorbers; Plessey fuel pumps; Dzus
     fasteners; Renold chains; Dunlop wheels, tyres and upholstery.
Engine
Engine.  Norton or J.A.P.       Carburettor:  Amal.
Fuel system:  Pressure feed by Plessey diaphragm pump, axle-driven with Bowden
     cable operation when on start or stationary.
Magneto:  Lucas or B.T.H.   Clutch:  Norton.     Gearbox:  Norton.
Weights and Dimensions
Unladen weight:  530 lb. (295 lb. front, 235 lb. rear).
Starting-line weight:  730 lb. (allowing 150 lb. for driver).   Distribution then
     approximately equal.
Wheelbase:  6ft.                          Overall length:  9ft. 10in.
Front track:  4ft                         Maximum height:  2ft. 6in.
Rear track:                               Maximum width (body):  3ft.
Frontal area:  6.25 sq. ft. including wheels and tyres.
Remarks:  Unusual features of car include front-wheel drive, inboard front
     brakes, shock-absorber and suspension in one unit (strut type) and quick-
     action knock-off wheels.
```

Fig 155

'brilliant engineer' by those who worked with him and a prolific and ingenious builder of motor racing specials. [37]. He had ambitions of building a Formula 1 car.

In 1953, he put an Aston-Martin engine into a new tubular chassis that he had constructed, with a neat body and characteristically small air intake. In 1956, Emeryson's Formula 1 car qualified for the British Grand Prix at Silverstone. It enjoyed some success, in particular with Roberta Cowell at the wheel in the 'Ladies' class' (Roberta Cowell's fascinating story is in Appendix II). By the end of 1959, Emery had also built a rear-engined Cooper-Connaught, again successfully raced by Roberta Cowell.

Twickenham was the home of Emeryson Cars from the late 1940s and through much of the 1950s. Initially the workshop was located in Campbell Road, Twickenham. The photograph *(fig 156)* of Emeryson Formula 3 500-8 was probably taken

Fig 156

outside the Emeryson Cars workshop in 1950/51.

During 1952, Paul Emery moved production to another workshop, in St. Margarets, at No.148, Amyand Park Road facing the railway line close to St. Margaret's Station *(see fig 146)*. Spanning the move, the production run of Emeryson F3 500 cars was contracted out to a motor workshop at Wythall in Worcestershire. The photograph *(fig 157)* shows that the Amyand Park Road site still had a motoring connection in 2020. The Campbell Road site however, is now occupied by a row of houses.

Paul Emery is one of just two racing-car constructors to have built cars for all four main Formulas: 1, 2, 3 and 4. Emeryson shares this accolade with one other manufacturer, motor racing giant Ferrari. The photograph *(fig 158)* shows Paul Emery driving a Formula 1 Emeryson-Alta at

Crystal Palace on 22nd May 1956, where he finished 2nd to Stirling Moss who was driving his own Maserati 250F. Emery said *'I built my own cars because I wanted to race and never had enough*

Fig 157

money to go racing except by building my own cars' **(37)**.

In 1957, Emeryson moved from Twickenham to larger premises in Camberley. In 1958, Paul Emery moved again to Guildford and then to Connaught's headquarters in Send, Surrey. There he built three F1

Fig 158

Emeryson-Maseratis that again achieved some success. Later, Emery developed Mini-based racing cars like the fibreglass bodied Emery Dart and Hillman Imp mid-engined Emery GT.

A number of Emeryson racing cars have survived, including five of the eight Emeryson 500 F3 cars that were constructed in the early 1950s. Mark Linstone owns one of these F3 cars which he prepared for racing in the 2021 season. His father, Cyril Linstone, worked with Paul Emery in his Twickenham workshops in the 1950s. Cyril helped the author with the details of this section in 2020, as did Duncan and Graham Rabagliati. Duncan owned Emeryson 500/7, now owned by Marek Reichmann, chief designer at Aston Martin. Another is owned by Jerry Greaves in the USA.

Bonhams sold a 1947 *'Emeryson Special'* for £20,125 in 2008, despite the vehicle not being independently verified.

Bonhams also offered the last surviving 1961 Emeryson-Climax' Formula 1 racing car restored in 2017 (see photograph *(fig 159)* which was sold at auction in 2020 for £161,000.

Fig 159

There is a piece of contemporary film of Roberta Cowell driving a Twickenham built Emeryson-Alta on the Brookland's Museum website (and YouTube): a *Pathe News* report entitled '*Roberta Cowell wins the 1957 Shelsley Walsh hill climb'*.

A familiar name to anyone living in Twickenham in the second half of the 20th century was Spikins because Spikins Garage was on a large and prominent site on Heath Road and later in Richmond Road. Willment was an equally familiar name. The Willment family's civil engineering company had been in business since the early 1900s. In 1957, Willment were responsible for building the Cooper Formula 1 Racing Team's new motor works in Surbiton. John Willment established his own garage in the 1950s and in 1962 decided to combine his rapidly expanding Ford dealership with his motor racing activities by creating a racing team to advertise the Willment brand.

Bob Spikins, his cars and Spikins Garage

A watchmaker by training, Frederick Robert George Spikins or Bob Spikins, was an avid motoring enthusiast who excelled in motorsport (racing, rallying, trialling & speed events) from the early 1920s through to 1951. He built several competition specials at Spikins Garages in Twickenham. These were his single-seater Singer known as The Bantam, a Hudson Special and the Laystall Cromard Special [38]. The Bantam was based on a 1933 Singer 9 Le Mans, transformed into a compact racer,

Fig 160

Fig 161a   *Fig 161b*

with a short wheelbase and underslung chassis fitted with a lightweight aluminium body. The Bantam can be seen in the photograph *(fig 160)* taken outside Spikins Heath Road premises in the mid 1930s. The Hudson Special could have gone into production and was offered by Spikins in an advertisement in the *Autocar,* 10th April 1936 *(fig 161a)*. Described as the 110 mph super charged Spikins Hudson Special, it was priced at £750 *(fig 161b)*. Perhaps surprisingly there were apparently no takers.

The Cromard, seen in the photograph *(fig 162)*, originally called the Spikins Special was financed by Laystalls in Wolverhampton where Spikins was chairman. It became known as the Laystall Cromard Special. Built in the late 1940s, it was based on an Amilcar chassis, but fitted with a 1.5-litre Lea-Francis racing engine. The Cromard competed at Goodwood in 1951 and went on to race in the 1951 Belgian Grand Prix. However Spikins was driving a Frazer Nash in this event so the Cromard was driven by his friend and colleague Basil de Mattos on Sunday 13 May 1951.

Fig 162

Fig 163

Tragically, Bob Spikins, driving the Frazer Nash, was involved in a five-car pile-up on the opening lap of the race. Aldo Gordini had lost control of his works Simca-Gordini T11 on a double bend. The race track was made up of a series of public roads in Chimay, near Charleroi. Spikins died almost immediately from the injuries that he had sustained in the accident. He was 51 years old. His wife and four-year old daughter Pauline were watching the race. An unimaginable loss for them but also for 1950s British motor racing. A week before his fatal crash, Bob Spikins finished a remarkable fourth in the One Hour Production Car race at Silverstone, driving the same Frazer Nash in which he would lose his life. As a result of the accident, the Cromard was never fully developed into the British Formula 2 car that it had seemed destined to be.

Spikins Garage remained a familiar sight in Heath Road, Twickenham for many more years, as a petrol station and local agent for a wide range of British marques, selling and servicing cars, as the advertisement shows *(fig 163)*. Spikins also took over the site with a long transport and motoring history at 5-11 Richmond Road, the former Corben's carriage factory (Chapter 6).

Amazingly, all three (known) Spikins Specials have survived:

- AMM 1 The Bantam based on the Singer is owned by Neil Thorp in the UK after spending some time in Australia.
- DRX 67 The Hudson Special also owned by Neil Thorp. Formerly CMP 1, it was owned in the 1940s by Paul Emery and reregistered when he sold it in 1948.
- The Spikins Special later known as the Laystall Cromard Special is now in Switzerland.

All the cars still take part in historic events.

Neil Thorp helped the author with the details of this section.

John Willment Automobiles

John Willment established a garage on the corner of the Chertsey Road and Whitton Road in Twickenham, which became known locally as *'Willment's Corner'*. It grew into one of the largest privately owned Ford main dealerships in the country. The site is still a garage today (2024), Toyota dealer Currie Motors.

John Willment had a passion for motor racing. The first car that he raced was a 100E Ford, with racing driver Jeff Uren. By 1962, he had established the Willment racing team. Willment Racing Division started to take shape in a workshop behind the garage *'in the shadows of the Twickenham Rugby Ground'*. Their slogan was *'Race-Proved by Willment'* [39] *(fig 164)*. He was able to combine his two businesses by racing Ford cars to advertise the garage. The photograph *(fig 165)* shows John Willment sitting at the wheel of an early prototype Willment car in the workshop.

Fig 164

Willment-Climax *'works cars'* were driven by Graham Hill and Jack Brabham in the 1950s. The photograph *(fig 166)* was taken at the Formule Libre race at the 1957 Brands Hatch, Boxing Day meeting. It shows a Willment sports/ racing car on the front row of the grid with Stuart

Fig 165

Fig 166

Lewis-Evans driving. Lewis-Evans also drove Formula 1 racing cars for Vanwall. The Willment-Climax LSL 893 of 1959 is shown in the photographs *(figs 167 and 168)*. Could this be the inspiration for the 1960s Batmobile?

Willment worked with many of the great racing car makers including Brabham, Lotus and local sports car manufacturer AC at Thames Ditton. Willment raced three AC Cobras, owned by

Figs 167 and 168

the American racing legend Carroll Shelby, at Le Mans and other European circuits in the early 1960s. Willment then developed its own Daytona Coupe CSX2131 based on Carroll Shelby's very successful Shelby Daytona Coupes. Willment team manager Jeff Uren recalled that *'it was built in the back of Obey's Garage in Twickenham'* [40]. The car came 7th in the 1963 Le Mans 24 hour race and in 1964, with Frank Gardner driving, won a number of British motor racing championships.

Towards the end of 1966, John Willment Race Shop took over production of the highly successful Ford GT40 from Ford Advanced Vehicles. His team won the Le Mans 24 hour race in 1968 and 1969. Both wins were in one of their Ford GT40s. Racing driver John Wyer joined Willment to form JWA - John Willment Automotive Engineering Ltd which could conveniently just as well be John Wyer Automotive Engineering Ltd, of course.

Willment was involved with F1, 2 and 3 cars as well as a host of other racing formulae. *Motor Sport* magazine described Willment as the largest private racing enterprise in Britain, working on up to nineteen cars at the same time for different races or events. John Willment Speed Shop was established, selling and fitting after-market accessories for *'boy racers'* wanting a piece of Willment's to customise their car.

Most Willment cars were adaptations of other manufacturers' models, often Fords, although they did produce a number of one-off racing cars at different times. Their only production model was a sports car with a tubular frame, light alloy body and a Coventry-Climax 1.5 litre engine. The transmission was of Willment's own design and included a five-speed gearbox.

A number of Willment or Willment modified cars have survived and come up for sale at auction from time to time. One sold at Bonhams in 2017 for £471,900.

Willment was winding down its motor racing operations in Twickenham by the 1970s. A number of former Willment employees set up their own motor racing enterprises in and around Twickenham. In the mid 1970s, David Price joined John Bracey, both former JWA employees, to form Bracey-Price Racing. The company based itself in the workshops at the rear of the former Obey's Garage at 113 Heath Road in Twickenham *(Fig 169)*. This site had previously also been used by John Willment Automobiles, mentioned above. Interestingly the site has transport connections that appear to go back much further, to the beginning of the 20th century or even earlier. Walter Biggs Coach builders had workshops there, before the property was numbered. By

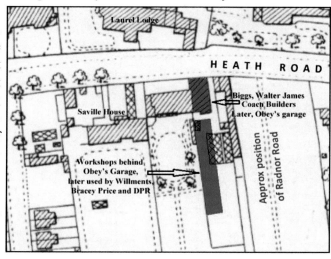

Fig 169

Fig 170

1915, a tyre maker was at the site and by c1922, former Tamplin's manager Frank Obey took over the premises. Obey's Garage closed in the 1960s, not long after Heath Road was widened in 1966. It then became a Heron petrol station, one of the first 'self-service' petrol stations run by Gerald Ronson. Today (2024), the site still has strong motoring connections, hosting the MKG3000 car dealership. The racing car heritage continued for a while, with the workshops being used to prepare Mazda MX5's for the race track. The workshops are now MKG's car service bays, as the 2022 photograph shows *(fig 170)*.

Two other JWA Racing Division employees had already set up in business together in Twickenham to produce motor racing engines. Their company, Racing Services Partnership occupied another site with a long transport and motoring history. It was part of Swan Island behind No.1 Strawberry Vale, shown on the 1934 map (also mentioned in Chapter 5) *(see fig 139)*. The probable location of '*Milham's Motor & Boat Building Works*', is also shown. Milham's boathouse is shown in the photograph taken c1910 *(fig 171)*. Writing on the boathouse is just visible, saying

Fig 171

'Harry Milham' between the windows at the top of the building, and the words *'Engineer'* and *'Launch'*. This strongly suggests that the boathouse was building motor launches or at least fitting launches with petrol engines. This site too has a motoring connection today (2024), as home to LJ Motorcycle dealership and repairs.

Bracey-Price and David Price Racing

David Price had joined John Bracey in the 1970's to form Bracey-Price Racing, as stated above. By 1976 Bracey-Price Racing had become David Price Racing (DPR) and was involved in a Formula 3 racing partnership with British Leyland (BL) through their Unipart division. Many future Formula drivers raced for the team, including Nigel Mansell, Martin Brundle, Johnny Dumphries and Tiff Needell. Andrew Ridgeley, formerly of pop duo Wham! joined DPR to race F3 cars in France, after Wham! split up. They used the Dolomite Sprint engine in the car, which achieved considerable success. Amongst the most notable was Nigel Mansell's win at the 1979 British Formula 3 championship.

DPR went on to prepare and race production BL cars like the TR7 V8 and the 3.5 litre Rover SD1. They were asked to develop a racing saloon car for BL. It was reported that… *'work on a prototype began at their Twickenham base… "Project Lassie" was born'* [41]. Later (2002), DPR assisted MG in the development of the *XPower SV*.

Bracey-Price and David Price Racing used the same site at the rear of the former Obey's Garage, in Heath Road Twickenham, as had been used by their former employee, John Willment. The site is shown *(see fig 169)* opening on to Heath Road (later numbered 113) when it was Biggs, Walter James Coach builders at about the same time as the photograph *(fig 172a)* was taken in 1904. It shows a leafy lane with large houses behind high walls particularly on the north side and the carriage works that became Obey's Garage half way down the road on the right. A detail from the photograph *(fig 172b)* reveals sign writing on the wall that reads 'Carriages built to Order'.

DPR adapted production cars, as Willment's had, but also Grand Prix racing cars. In 1979, they became involved in Formula 1. Giacomo

Fig 172a

Fig 172b

Agostini, champion Moto-GP rider, bought a pair of Williams FW06s using his Marlboro connections and asked David Price to head his racing team. In September 1979, Agostini sat on the grid at Imola with Niki Lauda, Gilles Villeneuve, Keke Rosberg and recently crowned F1 champion Jody Scheckter in the biggest race of his four-wheeled career [42]. Price had entered Agostini for the Imola race because *'Bernie (Ecclestone) twisted my arm... as he wanted bums on seats... (Agostini) did a really solid job'* [43].

Despite early success, Agostini didn't follow the likes of Surtees and Hailwood into a long Formula 1 career after moving from motorbikes. He retired as a racing driver in 1980. DPR continued to be involved in Formula 1 and Le Mans racing and remained at the forefront of the sport until at least 2012.

David Price died aged 75 in February 2023.

Racing Services Partnership

Ken Brittain and Spike Winter formed Racing Services in 1967. Initially they were sited at Aston Martin's old factory in Feltham, after Aston Martin had moved to Newport Pagnall. In 1971, they moved to Swan Island off Strawberry Vale *(see fig 139)*. Although not strictly a motor manufacturer, they did produce motor-racing engines. Spike Winter had previously managed the racing division for Willment after working for Frazer Nash. Ken Brittain had moved to Willment from Aston Martin. By 1973, cars powered by Racing Services engines were winning one event after another in all the motor racing categories in which they competed. *Motor Sport* magazine described them as *'prolific engine builders'* and very successful ones too [44].

The photograph *(fig 173)* shows Racing Services engineering workshop with John Miles, former Formula 1 racing driver for Lotus and BRM, working on an engine. Miles also raced Lotus Elans and Diva GTs for Willment. Their

Fig 173

workshop was later used by John Paul Jacques,

Fig 174

grandson of Robert Bamford. Robert Bamford is seen in the photograph *(fig 174)*, and his role at Teddington Motorcar and Launch Works was discussed in Chapter 8. He was the engineering genius behind the Bamford and Martin motoring partnership. Bamford and Martin's first car to carry the legendary Aston Martin badge was AM 4656 in 1915. Aston was named after the Aston Hill climb where it had competed. The car was heavily used in the First World War and earned the unflattering nick name, *'Coal Scuttle'*. It did, however, achieve

Figs 175 and 176

notable success after the war at the Brooklands circuit and elsewhere and set Aston Martin on the road to motoring success.

The Racing Services Logo in the photograph *(fig 175)*, has survived inside a toolbox lid. The toolbox could still be found in John's workshop in March 2020, as the photograph *(fig 176)* shows. The building opposite the workshop housed Racing Services *'Engine Dynamometer'* for testing their engines' power output, now part of LJ Motorcycles.

The Costin-Nathan car

In August 2019, Eel Pie Island Museum received an email from Roger Nathan asking if the museum would be interested in finding out more about the Costin-Nathan racing car. This highly successful racing car of the 1960s was constructed around a wooden monocoque made at George Sim's boatyard on Eel Pie Island. Sim's boatyard was already building high-tech wooden rowing eights for both the Oxford and Cambridge Universities boat-race teams at the time.

Roger Nathan made his name in the early 1960s racing Lotus Elites with great success. Nathan provided the driving skills and worked on the highly tuned 1000cc Hillman Imp engine. Frank Costin provided the car's design and ultra-light construction. Although he borrowed from his earlier experience, the end result was really quite revolutionary.

The photographs *(figs 177 a/b)* show the wooden dashboard, part of the wooden monocoque and, attached to the front and rear of the monocoque, the light-weight tubular steel space frame. Roger Nathan recalled that *'each monocoque took a carpenter six weeks to make and cost us £500'.* [45]. The prototype had aluminium nose and rear body sections made by Williams and Pritchard in Edmonton. The subsequent production cars had fibreglass body sections made by the same company.

The Costin brothers, Frank and Mike, were at the forefront of post-war British motor racing. While Frank was with Lotus he was responsible for, arguably, some of the finest Lotus sports cars. After Lotus, he formed Marcos with Jem Marsh (MARsh/COStin). Brother

Figs 177a and 177b

Mike with Keith Duckworth formed Cosworth (COStin/duckWORTH), one of the sport's foremost engine makers. Of course they could have called the company TinDuck!

Around twenty Costin-Nathans were produced in GT and open cockpit form. Nathan raced the prototype throughout 1966 with great success and almost without the usual teething problems that racing cars experience. The car proved particularly successful at the Coupes de Paris in September. Roger Nathan recalls *'we went to scrutineering... people saw it was wooden and started laughing! In particular the Abarth team... here I was, an Englishman, 22 years old with his own wooden car up against the might of Fiat!'* Nathan continued... *'(they) were not laughing... when I gained fastest time and thus pole position on the starting grid. I just managed to get in front of the works Abarth into the first right hand corner after the start of the race and won the race outright '*[46]. The outraged Abarth team then claimed a technical irregularity with the Costin-Nathan but were overruled.

Fig 178

Roger Nathan recalled that *'in 1967 he produced a GT version with some limited sponsorship from BP and Rootes Group who were about to be purchased by the Chrysler Corporation'* [47]. A Costin-Nathan GT can be seen at a motor show with a *'Powered by Rootes'* slogan on the door, a reference to its Hillman Imp based engine *(fig 178)*.

Fig 179

Nathan recalled that the Costin-Nathan, later renamed the Nathan-Astra, won every national and international event in which it was entered between 1966 and 1970. The photograph shows a GT passing the chequered flag *(fig 179)*.

'The GT was raced at the International Le Mans 24 hour race in that year. Unfortunately the car was only finished just before the event and was rushed to Le Mans after a single test day that proved very promising.

However, fate had different ideas… an intermittent misfire [47]. This was found to be a fault in the aircraft quality wiring that couldn't be rectified.

The prototype Costin-Nathan was recently restored by Roger Nathan in an epic three-year programme and the car is now on indefinite loan to the National Motor Museum at Beaulieu *(fig 180)*, though Nathan plans to take the car back out on to the track again for selected events.

Roger Nathan still remembers the finger bruising experience of carrying the finished wooden monocoques from George Sim's boatyard - two people inching their way across the little footbridge from Eel Pie Island to Twickenham Embankment, their valuable cargo just millimetres away from the sides of the bridge.

Eel Pie Island had found its way back into Britain's motoring history and Twickenham's motorcars had come full circle, back to where it all began so many years earlier.

Appendix I. Henry Cornelius Hunter,

MY GREAT GRANDFATHER

HENRY CORNELIUS HUNTER *(fig 181)*, my great grandfather, moved to Twickenham c1895 when he was 30 years old. He was already an experienced boatbuilder and marine draughtsman. He had been working in the trade from the age of 14 in Faversham, Kent. The family had worked as shipwrights for generations. His father was a journeyman-carpenter joiner, building wooden-hulled boats at the boatyard where Henry found his first job.

After the boatyard in Faversham, Henry moved to Southampton, no doubt to broaden his experience and widen his skills. Southampton had a long history of shipbuilding and by the late nineteenth century was already a flourishing port. At that time a fifth dry-dock for ship repair was being built, the largest in the world. Here he would have gained experience of working on steel-hulled steam ships.

Fig 181

Henry would have been attracted to Twickenham by the pioneering work taking place on Eel Pie Island. Not long after he had moved to Twickenham, he married Rosa Jane who lived in nearby Isleworth. They rented No.8 Sion Road, almost opposite the site on Eel Pie Island where William Sargeant had his boathouse. Sargeant himself lived a few doors away at No.2 Sion Road. Sargeant's company, The Thames Electric and Steam Launch Company, was pioneering the building of electric launches on the Thames. His extensive boatyard, workshops and slipway can be seen on the c1898 map *(fig 182)* and photograph *(refer to fig 4)*. Interestingly Moritz Immisch had also been building electric boats just a few miles upstream on Platt's Eyot at Hampton since 1889.

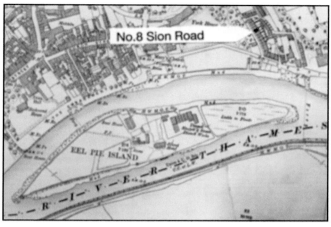

No.8 Sion Road

Fig 182

Henry was a boat builder and 'Naval Architect', having worked his way up through the boat building trade. It is known that Henry worked on river launches in Twickenham and by the 1911 Census *(fig 183)*, he was a 'Motor' and Marine engineer. Henry had combined the skills he'd gained working on boats with the new motor engineering technology being pioneered in Twickenham.

Whilst researching Twickenham's motorcars, my sister discovered a treasure trove of our great grandfather's things from the 1900s, that had been kept by our father until his death in 2006. It is not only a fascinating

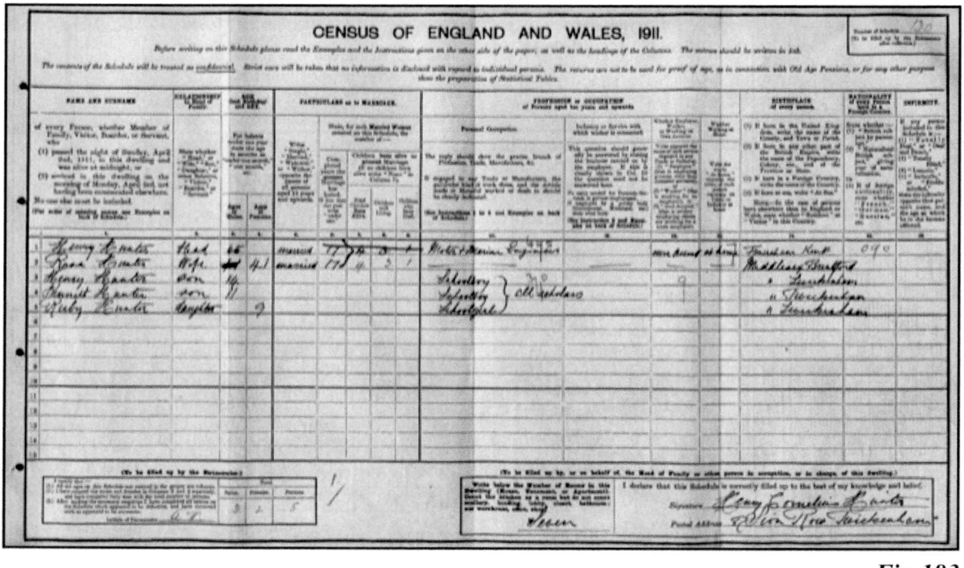

CENSUS OF ENGLAND AND WALES, 1911.

Fig 183

archive of the suppliers of parts to the motor industry, that were used in the construction of the Orleans cars, but a wonderful collection of catalogues from their competitors in the 1900s *(figs 184a/b/c)*. There is also a letter to Van Toll & Co. Ltd. from The Aster Engineering

Fig 184a

Company, one of their suppliers. It is dated late in 1910, the year that Orleans Motors went into liquidation *(fig 185)*. It seems clear that Henry was closely associated with The Orleans car company by the 1900s.

Figs 184b/c

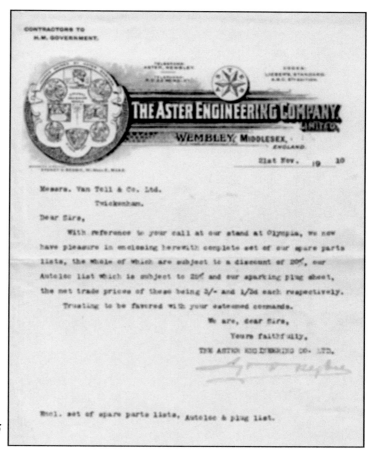

Fig 185

Johannes van Toll, had left the Orleans business by then and was establishing the motor and marine engineering company, Van Toll, Mayer & Co. at 93, Richmond Road. This would undoubtedly have been attractive to Henry, ideally combining his marine and motor engineering skills and perhaps continuing his association with van Toll.

Henry bought a small parcel of land in Orleans Road, close to the engineering works on the corner of Chapel Road, discussed in Chapter 3. He built garages on the land that my father remembered were used for storing different types of motorcar and cycle components.

Fig 186 *(above)*

Fig 187 *(left)*

The photograph *(fig 186)* of Orleans Road looking south at about that time, shows housing on the west side of the road, since demolished. The land on which he built garages was just beyond the houses. Today, garages run right along that side of Orleans Road, as the photograph taken in 2018 shows *(fig 187)*.

After the closure of the Orleans factory in 1910 and the death of van Toll in 1913, Henry may have worked with one of the other motorcar manufacturers nearby, ordering and supplying motor parts. Twickenham Motor Company had opened in Richmond Road, a hundred yards from Sion Road.

Henry turned his motor engineering skills to aircraft manufacture, which was becoming established locally. Henry's archive supports this as it contains a detailed blueprint of an aircraft design. It would seem likely that during the First World War, Henry's engineering skills were put to use in Twickenham's newly established aircraft industry. WGC Hayward & Co. at the Beaufort Works, just off Richmond Road, became involved in secret government work for the fledgling aircraft industry during the war. Hayward's were *'charged with work of the highest importance... of great value to the nation'.*[48]

Motorcars had captured Henry's imagination as a driver too and he became one of Twickenham's earliest motorists. *'I was one of the first men in Twickenham to own a motorcar',* he would tell my father when he was a boy. It was quite unusual for a working man to own a car in the early days of motoring and some time before motoring became a realistic aspiration for the working class, rather than the preserve of the affluent Toads of Toad Hall. This was, of course, an aspiration that the makers of Twickenham's motorcars did their best to make a reality.

One incident from Henry's early days as a motorist is recorded, but shows him perhaps not in the best possible light. In a newspaper report in *The Daily Telegraph and Courier* on 12th May 1905, Henry was fined *'twenty shillings and costs'* at Brentford Magistrates' Court for *'driving a motor-tricycle to the common danger of the public'.* The speed limit on public highways had been raised to 20 mph by the Motor Car Act of 1903, but remained lower in towns. Previously the speed limit had been 14 mph and before 1896 just 2 mph in towns. The Act also made car registration and displaying a registration number-plate compulsory. Driving licences were introduced too, though it was not until 1935 that it was necessary to take a driving test.

Clearly speed was a contentious issue. Like other towns, Twickenham would have introduced its own speed limit by 1905. Henry was accused of driving *'through a congested part of Twickenham on the wrong side [of the road] when hundreds of foot passengers were returning from church and from the river. His speed was stated to be fifteen or sixteen miles an hour and he knocked down a little boy who had to receive medical attention'.*

The motor tricycle Henry was driving was probably a De Dion-Bouton, the most popular motor vehicle in Europe at the turn of the twentieth century. Produced from 1897 to 1905, it had a single cylinder four-stroke engine which is considered to be the forerunner of the modern motorcycle engine. In 1900 De Dion-Bouton was the largest car manufacturer in the world. Their cars were hand-made in France at Puteaux near Paris, though some were made in the UK under licence.

Early in 1907, Henry was turning his attention to motorcycling. Motorcycle manufacture had yet to arrive in Twickenham, so Henry was interested in the first motorbikes being produced by the Triumph Cycle Co. *(fig 188)*. They sent him their *'preliminary list of Motor Cycles, our full catalogue not being ready'*. They offered him a motor trade discount of 10% and another 2.5% off for cash *(fig 189)*.

Henry became a motorcyclist but with tragic consequences for his wife Rosa. My father recalled that he had only ever seen his grandmother in bed at No.8, Sion Road. She had apparently been involved in a serious

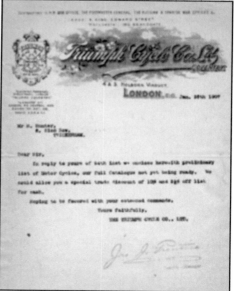

Fig 188

Fig 189

motorcycle accident. She was badly injured and became bedridden for the rest of her life. She died in 1931 aged sixty-two.

The photograph *(fig 190)* was taken outside No.8 Sion Road in 1916, shows Henry with Rosa and daughter Ruby, aged fourteen.

Henry Cornelius Hunter died in Twickenham in 1949, aged eighty-two. He still owned No.8 Sion Road and the garages in Orleans Road.

Fig 190

Appendix II. Twickenham motor racing driver, Roberta Cowell

MOTOR RACING DRIVER, Roberta Cowell, was born Robert Cowell, son of Major-General Sir Ernest Cowell, in 1918. Cowell served as a front-line Spitfire pilot in the Second World War, incredibly surviving blacking out at 31,000 feet because of oxygen starvation: the Spitfire continued flying itself for an hour or more through German anti-aircraft fire. Regaining semi-consciousness at low level, Cowell landed the Spitfire safely at RAF Gatwick. In October 1944 Cowell was shot down, crash landed, captured and imprisoned by the Germans. Cowell escaped twice, was recaptured, and eventually liberated by the *Red Army*.

In 1948, Cowell separated from his wife and revealed that *'my unconscious mind was predominantly female'*.[49] They'd had two children together before the war. Cowell became close friends with Michael Dillon, a British doctor who was the first man to have gender surgery. In 1951 Cowell had gender surgery performed by Sir Harold

Fig 191

Gillies, widely considered to be the father of plastic surgery. Once news of her gender reassignment broke, it received world-wide attention. Roberta Cowell was the first known trans woman in Britain to undergo such surgery.

Cowell is seen driving a super-charged Emerson-Alta racing car in the photograph *(fig 191)*. She set a new ladies record at the Shelsley Walsh hill climb in September 1957 with a time of 40.41 seconds. Roberta then professed the ambition *'to lead her own team of women drivers in the Le Mans 24-hour sports-car classic'* [50]. She remained active in British motor racing until the 1970s.

Roberta Cowell moved into sheltered accommodation in Hampton in the 1990s though continued to own and drive powerful cars. Her cars were always serviced at Alderson's Garage in Station Road, owner Dave Anderson recalled.[51] She died in October 2011, unpublicised as she had requested and not reported until 2013.

Roberta Cowell's story, virtually forgotten until recently, is receiving renewed interest. Articles about her have appeared in the press recently, including major articles in the *Guardian, Telegraph, Independent, Daily Mail* and the *New York Times*.

APPENDIX III. NEW ORLEANS CARS STILL IN

EXISTENCE

ALMOST EVERY YEAR since 1927 at least one New Orleans Voiturette has taken part in the London to Brighton Veteran Car Run. This is testimony to the resilience and enduring appeal of this little car. This number increased to two or three cars after the Second World War. Then, from the mid 1950s, three and sometimes four New Orleans cars have taken part. An extract from the *'Commemoration Run List of Entrants'* for 4th November 1956 *(fig 192)* shows four New Orleans cars participating. All were Voiturettes from 1900.

VETERAN CAR RUN. List of Entrants—continued.

No.	Vehicle	Year	No. of Cyls.	H.P.	Body	Entrant	Driver (if other than Entrant)
40°	DE DION BOUTON	1900	1	4½	Voiturette	J. A. G. Burchell	Entrant or D. E. Green
41	DE DION BOUTON	1900	1	3½	Quadricycle	Hanns Georg School	
42°	GARDNER-SERPOLLET STEAMER	1900	4	5	Double Phaeton	Alec Hodsdon	
43°	GEORGES RICHARD	1900	2	9	Dog Cart	James E. Crossman	
44°	M.M.C.	1900	2	6	Tonneau	Ernest Hare	
45°	NEW ORLEANS	1900	2	7	Voiturette	Sir Clive Edwards	Entrant and C. R. D. Thomas
46°	NEW ORLEANS	1900	1	3½	Voiturette	Gerald S. Sanders	
47	NEW ORLEANS	1900	1	3½	Voiturette	J. M. Schofield	Entrant and J. Schofield
48°	NEW ORLEANS	1900	1	3½	Voiturette	D. G. Silcock	M. Rowe
49°	PEUGEOT	1900	2	8	Double Phaeton	H. E. F. Parkinson	
50°	PIEPER	1900	1	3½	Voiturette	William Vaux	
51	ALBION	1901	2	8	Dog Cart	Albion Motors Ltd.	Ken Wharton
52°	BENZ	1901	1	4½	Two Seater	Wilfrid Andrews	
53°	CLEMENT-PANHARD	1901	1	4½	Voiturette	Major James C. France	

Fig 192

In the 2018 Run, held on 3rd November, there were four New Orleans cars entered, all dating from 1900. Three were single-cylinder 3.5 hp models but the fourth was a 14hp twin-cylinder model, registration number 8710 MN, the only surviving twin-cylinder example. The car was formally registered AX 74 and participated in the run on numerous occasions with its original registration number. The change in registration number took place when the car was exported to the Isle of Man in 1945. The Milntown Trust at Milntown House, Lezayre near Ramsey owns and maintains the car. A profile, written by Andrew Kelsey who maintains the car for the trust, follows below. They proudly reported that, *'this was the 31st time that the car had participated in the run'*.

List of New Orleans Voiturettes known to be in existence today:

- Chassis No. 7 Engine No. 27 single cylinder 3.5 hp 1900 Reg. F 1254
- Chassis No. 8 Engine No. 16 single cylinder 3.5 hp 1900 Reg. EW 113
- Chassis No.12 Engine No. 6   single cylinder 3.5 hp 1900 Reg. SX 13
- Chassis No.76 Engine No/Nos.? twin cylinder 7 hp 1900 Reg. AX 74 / 8710 MN
- Chassis No.77 Engine No. ?   single cylinder 3.5 hp 1900/1 Reg. H 17

Fig 193

Unfortunately registration numbers are of little use in establishing the date of manufacture of any of these cars. All are believed to have been built in 1900. Chassis No's. 76 and 77, either late 1900 and very early in 1901.

SX 13 and AX 74 were registered on 1st January 1904, the first day that all cars had to be registered and carry registration numbers. The Motor Car Act of 1903 made this compulsory for the first time. F 1254 was registered by the Essex Record Office but not until late in 1904. EW 113 must have been *re*registered, as the Huntingdonshire registration number that it carries wasn't issued until at least 1908. H 17's date of registration is unknown, as Middlesex records did not survive [52].

The two photographs show the same car, Voiturette AX 74 *(fig 193)* in the 1950s and later reregistered 8710 MN *(fig 194)*.

Fig 194

Fig 195

Fig 196

Paul Edwards can be seen in the photograph *(fig 195)* at the end of the 2019 London to Brighton Veteran Car Run, driving SX13 across the finishing line in Madeira Drive in Brighton.

EW 113, New Orleans Voiturette Chassis No.8 above, returned to Twickenham briefly in 1981, to be exhibited at the *'May Fair'* on May 23rd that year. It can be seen photographed in the *Surrey Comet* with Mrs Elsie van Toll at the wheel, Johannes's daughter-in-law *(fig 196)*. The car was owned at the time by Edward Curtis of South Benfleet in Essex.

Two profiles of surviving New Orleans cars, provided by their current owner/keeper, follow:

New Orleans Voiturette SX 13

With chassis No.12 and engine No.6, SX 13 is probably the earliest surviving Voiturette from the Orleans Works, Twickenham in 1900. The car is now in the hands of Paul Edwards, who maintains it in his garage at home. He drives it in the summer months and participates almost every November in the London to Brighton Veteran Car Run.

His father bought the car in 1953 for the sum of £35, as the receipt *(fig 197)* shows (that is around £1000 in today's money). It was just a collection of parts but it came with the crucial paperwork to prove the car's provenance. It also came with other original documents. He transported the parts home on the back of his vintage Morris car in and on top of the rear dickie seat.

As the receipt shows, SX 13 was bought from a Mr. J H White, apparently of the *'R White and Sons'* family, lemonade and ginger beer manufacturer of Camberwell. White had bought the car from a garage proprietor, Bob Bates of Seal in Kent. The previous owner had bought SX 13 from a car dealer, Mr Amery, who had acquired it as a left over from a property

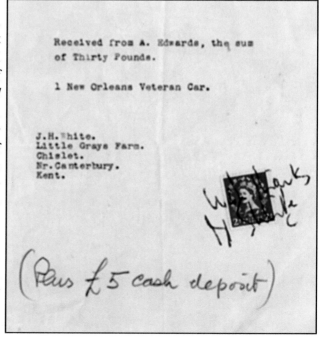

Fig 197

clearance. The property being cleared was that of Mr. Frappel of Meadowcroft on Westerham Hill in Kent, who had recently died. Amery found the remains of the car on the property. Paul Edwards believes that Frappel was the original owner of SX 13, who used it for going to market and also for powering his bench saw! This would have been an easy adaptation for a belt driven car like the Voiturette. Thus, in over 120 years on the road, SX 13 had had only four or five owners, when Paul took possession of the car from his father Alan in 2008.

Alan Edwards started to restore the car in the 1960s. However the full restoration wasn't completed until 1996, when Paul helped his father complete the project. In 1996, SX13 was entered for its first London to Brighton Veteran Car Run (LBVCR). On that occasion, it didn't manage to finish the 54 mile journey from Hyde Park, making it only as far as Buckingham Palace! So they set about rebuilding the 3.5 hp single-cylinder engine, completing the job in 1998.

In the year 2000, marking the car's 100th anniversary, Paul and his father again attempted the LBVCR… this time successfully. The photograph *(fig 198)* shows them crossing Westminster Bridge in the early hours of the morning. SX 13 has participated almost every year since and completing the course on just about every occasion. Paul can be seen *(fig 199)* driving SX 13 along Marine Drive in Brighton at the end of the Run with his wife Jo and son Tom and in 2016 with Tom at the wheel, the next generation to love SX 13 *(fig 200)*. Note the SX 13 hats.

Fig 198

Fig 199

Fig 200

Paul has dedicated the car to his father Alan, who died in 2008, aged 83. The brass plaque attached to the front of the car reads: *'To live in the hearts you leave behind is not to die'*. Quoted from the 1825 poem *Hallowed Ground* by Scottish poet Thomas Campbell *(fig 201)*.

Fig 201

He will also live on in that little piece of motoring history that he rescued in 1953.

The 'Manx' twin cylinder New Orleans 8710 MN.

Writen by Andrew Kelsey, who maintains 8710 MN at the Thomas Collection of historical vehicles at Milntown House and gardens on the Isle of Man.

The only twin-cylinder New Orleans Voiturette known to exist, now resides on the Isle of Man.

It is the oldest vehicle in the Thomas Collection of historical vehicles at Milntown House and gardens and the oldest car on the Island.

A small team of volunteer mechanics keep the vehicle in full running order and successfully entered it in the 2018 London to Brighton Run.

Milntown visitors are often surprised to learn that despite its name , it has no American connections whatsoever and that it was made in Twickenham in 1900.

The first owners of this car were Herbert and Amy Hartland who lived at Hardwick Court in Monmouthshire. When car registrations in Britain began in 1904, it was given the number AX 74. The Hartland's gardener kept the car in regular use for the next forty years.

During the war, Sir Clive Edwards, who came from a South Wales steel making family, was stationed in Bicester where he met fellow soldier and motor cycle enthusiast and engineer Bob Thomas. In 1944, Sir Clive bought the New Orleans from Mrs Hartland's estate and it was transported on an army lorry to his billet at the Old Workhouse in Bicester.

With Bob's skilled help, it was restored in time for them to enter the first London to Brighton Run after the war in 1946. Petrol rationing prevented the run in 1947, but Clive and Bob were to go on to enter the car over thirty times.

Madeira Drive in Brighton must be a welcome sight after a 62 mile journey on a wet November day in a vehicle that lacks even the most rudimentary weather protection, as the photograph *(fig 202)* shows.

The odd problem did occasionally arise, but the little car always got to Brighton - a remarkable record that remains intact up to and including the latest run in 2018.

The most serious and challenging problem occurred in 1948. With Brighton just 20 miles away, disaster struck.

Sir Clive relates that whilst he was at the wheel... *'There was an ominous clonk from number 2 cylinder'*. They discovered that... *'the crankshaft had broken clean in two'*.

Fig 202

At the side of the road, a very skilled and determined Bob Thomas managed to convert the twin cylinder engine into a functioning one cylinder engine for them to continue on their way to Brighton. The photograph *(fig 203)* shows a determined Bob Thomas driving on with the broken crankshaft. Sir Clive follows in a Lea Francis *"woody"* and a trailer. The distinction of being the only car to have completed the LBVCR with a broken crankshaft remains unchallenged.

Fig 203

Clive has recorded that Lea Francis made a new crankshaft for the car for … *'not too many pots of gold'*.

In 1963, Sir Clive Edwards, his mother Kathleen and Bob Thomas took their growing collection of cars and motorcycles and emigrated to the Isle of Man, buying the historic Milntown house and 15 acre estate. AX 74 now acquired a new Manx registration number… 8710 MN.

When Sir Clive died, his friend Bob Thomas established Milntown House with its gardens and vehicle collection as a charitable trust. Subsequently when Bob died, the entire estate was bequeathed to the Manx nation.

The mechanical specifications

Automotor magazine published a road test of the twin-cylinder on 6th October 1900. The timing cam for the ignition is on the outer end of the left-hand cylinder. Each cylinder is 850 cc in capacity The photograph *(refer to Fig 10b)* shows the air-cooled transverse engine made from two engines joined by the flywheel.

This long-stoke engine with its large flywheel provides a good deal of torque and although it has only two forward gears, they are quite high gears. Once under way it is a brisk performer.

Clive Edward wrote … *'in good conditions maximum speed is 38-40 mph and cruising 25-30 mph with acceleration to match'.*

The drive from the engine flywheel is transmitted from a segmented wooden pulley attached to the flywheel, then to the gearbox and rear axle by means of a crossed leather transmission belt. At the rear, the belt can be made to run on one of two pulleys. One is a free running idler pulley and the other is fixed to the driveshaft which turns the input shaft to the gears.

To move off, a gear is selected with the use of the clutch pedal. As the belt is slid across from the freely spinning idler pulley onto the fixed pulley *'land'* it begins to turn the shaft and the car moves forwards. This type of flat belt drive system was used extensively in thousands of factories at that time to operate all sorts of machinery and known as the *'fast and loose'* flat belt drive system (the *'fast'* pulley transmitted the drive and the *'loose'* pulley was the idle pulley).

Mechanics were therefore very familiar with it. It was easily repaired and considered very reliable. These features were promoted in Burford and Van Toll's advertising as was the successful completion of the 1900 *'1000 mile reliability run'*.

Another mechanical feature is the extensive use of ball bearings both in the wheel hubs and in the transmission. This too was drawing on established engineering, as the Birmingham-made mass produced bearings were used world-wide in the bicycle industry.

The braking system

The braking system consists of a foot brake, a hand brake and a pivoted rod that can be released to dig into the road surface to prevent the car rolling backwards on hills!

The foot brake (the left hand foot pedal) operates a band-type brake on the end of the transmission drive shaft. There is a limitation with this system – if the gears are in neutral and the drive shaft freely spinning, the foot brake has no effect and heavy application whilst in gear may stall the engine.

The handbrake operates expanding-shoe brakes on each rear wheel. The problem here is that, though effective in forward direction, they are of no use if the car is going backwards. This combination can be dangerous if slowing or stopping, or stalling on a hill, as there is the potential for the vehicle to run away backwards down the gradient.

The answer is the pivoted rod called a *'sprag'* or *'devil'* that can be lowered before the ascent of a hill and dragged along the ground. In the event of the car reversing, the *sprag* would readily dig into the rough road surface and so stop the car from running back down the slope.

The lighting system

The lighting system depends on two elegant Belgian single candle lamps *(fig 204)*. The candles are in spring loaded holders so, as the candle

burns down, the spring pushes the candle upwards to compensate. This maintains the flames position at the focal point of a very powerful convex glass lens. It gives quite a surprising amount of light.

Milntown's New Orleans is a fascinating, working Victorian motorcar for which the term *'horseless carriage'* is very appropriate as it was made in the earliest days of motoring history.

Fig 204

It has yet a further distinction. After the Hartlands, Sir Clive, Bob and the Trust that they established, have been the only owners, making this New Orleans arguably a 120 year old two-owner car!

NEW ORLEANS

VOITURETTE.

BURFORD. VAN TOLL AND CO.,

TWICKENHAM.

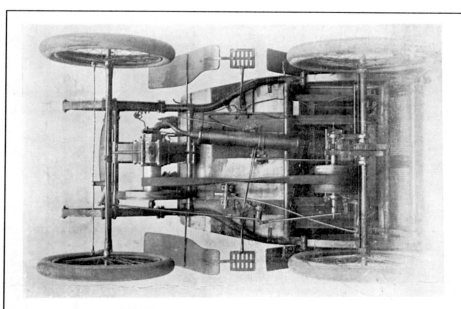

The accompanying illustrations show the outward appearance and internal economy of the Orleans voiturette. There are four points in connection with the motor, viz., the simple method of attaching the cylinder to the crank chamber, the means by which access is quickly obtained to the induction and exhaust valves, the manner of cooling the cylinder and piston from the crank chamber, and the simple type of carburetter employed, which all deserve illustration and description. The points which the designers of this car have kept most rigidly before

each. The motor is three and a half horse-power, with electric ignition, and cooled by means of a fan driven from the periphery of the flywheel, which effectively cools the cylinder, even when running at the slowest speed. The drive from the four-inch metal pulley and motorshaft is transmitted to the countershaft by a two-inch crossed belt. On the countershaft are three 7¾in. built wood pulleys, that on the left hand side being the fast speed, the centre the loose, and that on the right hand the slow speed pulley. The last named is carried on the countershaft, and the fast speed

Fig. 1.—Longitudinal Section of Crank Chamber.

them are strength, simplicity, and cheapness of construction, and so well have they succeeded that we are able to put these cars on the market at £130.

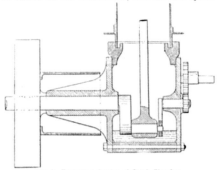

Fig. 2.—Transverse Section of Crank Chamber.

pulley on a sleeve, upon which the loose pulley runs. The two speeds are obtained, as can ... seen by the spur and pinion gear wheels ———— are always in mesh. The spur wheels surrou .... differential gear. The above arrangement is easily followed by a glance at the first illustration on preceding page, which is from a photograph of the underside of the car, the car having been reared up on end for the purpose.

The cars have two speeds, six and a half miles and sixteen miles, and are fitted with two brakes.

Reference to fig. 1, showing a longitudinal section of the crank chamber, enables the reader to perceive the means by which the internal cooling of the cylinder and piston is obtained. The ports A B are each closed by an outer and inner diaphragm of fine gauze T T, T T. Crank and cylinder lubrication is obtained in a simple, but thoroughly efficient, manner. It will be seen that the

Fig. 3.   Details of Valves and Attachment.   Fig. 4.

chase C, in which the open end of the cylinder rests, is twice the width necessary, and that at the end of each downward stroke the rim of the piston D dips into the channel. This channel is always kept full of oil, which is picked up at every stroke of the piston, and distributed over bearings and cylinder walls in a ceaseless shower. The oil also forms an oilbath F at the bottom of the crank chamber in the usual way. Fig. 2 is a transverse section of the crank chamber, showing at a glance the manner in which the crank is formed and the driving pulley carried. None of these diagrams must be taken as showing exactitude of detail, but they serve to make the system of construction comprehensible.

The front view, which is from a photograph of the fore end of the car with the motor bonnet removed, shows the cramp or dog over the cylinder, which holds down the cylinder head on to the cylinder barrel and the cylinder barrel into the faced circular chase (fig. 1). By simply unscrewing the large setscrew bearing upon the top of the combustion chamber, and loosening the eye bolts, and detaching the induction and exhaust, the cramp can be

Fig. 5.—Elevation of Carburetter.

turned down and the cylinder head and barrel dismounted rapidly and easily. The base of the motor bonnet slides in grooves in the wooden carriage, and is held in position by one butterfly nut only. Figs. 3 and 4 show the manner in which by the two fang bolts B B the induction and exhaust valve cases are secured to the projection cast in part with the cylinder head. The nuts A A are loosened, and the bolts removed laterally, giving immediate access to both valves. In case of mishap new valves can be put into position in a very short space of time.

Fig. 5 is an elevation and fig. 6 a cross section of the carburetter, which is about as simple and as cheap to make as it well can be. T is the petrol supply pipe, A the distributer, and B the vaporising chamber. D is a strip of felt, cut into small strips, which, when the cylinder charges and the air is drawn through the chamber B, are presumed to flap about therein as shown in fig. 6. The petrol soaks into the felt from the petrol distributer A, and a large area of petrol-soaked felt is thus offered for carburation.

The motor is securely and simply carried by six bolted brackets on a strong tubular rectangular steel

Front View of New Orleans Car with Motor Bonnet removed.

frame (the longitudinal tubes being 1⅝in. in diameter and twelve gauge, and the transverse tubes 1⅝in. and fourteen gauge), upon which the body, strongly but lightly made, is mounted. The whole car weighs about four hundredweight.

The New Orleans car, too, is fitted with a simple and ingenious method of taking up the slack of the belt by means of a lever placed conveniently in front of the driver.

Fig. 6.—Section of Carburetter.

Appendix V. The Orleans Motor Co. Ltd.
Catalogue c1907

THE

ORLEANS MOTOR CO.
LIMITED.

30-40 h.p. Four Cylinder Car.

CARLTON HOUSE, 11c, REGENT STREET, S.W.
AND
ORLEANS WORKS, TWICKENHAM, MIDDLESEX.

Telegrams: "ORLEANAUTO, LONDON."
"MOTORS, TWICKENHAM."

Telephones: 1533 GERRARD.
92 RICHMOND.
325 P.O. RICHMOND.

TRIALS AT ANY TIME.

CHIEF CHARACTERISTICS OF

30-40 h.p. 4-Cylinder and
35-45 h.p. 6-Cylinder : : ORLEANS CARS

ENGINES. The Engines have their Water Jacket and Cylinders cast in one piece.

The Four-Cylinder Model has its Cylinders cast in pairs, with all the Valves on the same side of the engine.

The Six-Cylinder Model has its Cylinders cast separately, the Valves being placed on opposite sides of the engine.

BEARINGS. The Bearings are designed with a large amount of wearing surface, oil being supplied by means of a pump which forces the oil through a hollow crank shaft.

View of Crank Shaft.

The Crank Shaft is turned from a nickel-steel forging, and runs in five anti-friction bearings.

The top ends of the connecting rods and the gudgeon pins are of hardened steel.

The bottom ends are of anti-friction metal, and are adjustable.

The connecting rods are nickel-steel stampings.

GEAR BOX. The Gear Box has four speeds forward and reverse, direct drive being on the third speed. One great feature we have introduced is in regard to the pitch of the gears. These are of larger pitch than is usually found in similar type cars. Ball bearings are fitted throughout.

CLUTCH. The Clutch is of our patent inside cone type, which allows the whole of the clutch to be removed in a few minutes without dismounting any other part of the car. The cone is in two parts, enabling each half to be taken out by unscrewing four screws.

CHIEF CHARACTERISTICS OF

30-40 h.p. 4-Cylinder and
35-45 h.p. 6-Cylinder : : **ORLEANS CARS**

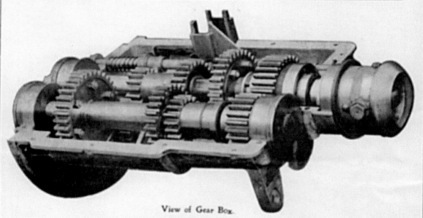

View of Gear Box.

LUBRICATION. The method of Lubrication is by means of a pump, which is driven off the cam shaft. The pump takes the oil from the reservoir at the bottom of the crank chamber and forces it up through the oil pipe, passing through a small cylinder containing a piston. The pressure of the oil forces up this piston and passes through a series of passages, connected with each of the bearings of the crank shaft. Should the oil pressure fail from any reason, the piston falls in the cylinder, making contact and ringing an electric bell.

The pressure of the oil delivered can be regulated by a Spring Valve in a byepass, which allows any excess of oil pumped to return to the reservoir.

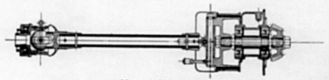

View of Cardan Shaft.

A special feature of the Cardan Shaft is that it can be taken out without removing any other part of the car.

BRAKES. There are three double acting metal to metal brakes, the foot brake operating on the end of the Cardan Shaft, while the other two act on the back wheels ; these being of the internal expansion type.

CHIEF CHARACTERISTICS OF

30-40 h.p. 4-Cylinder and
35-45 h.p. 6-Cylinder : : **ORLEANS CARS**

CLUTCH. The clutch is of our patent inside cone type, which allows the whole of the clutch to be removed in a few minutes without dismounting any other part of the car. The cone is in two parts, enabling each half to be taken out by unscrewing four screws.

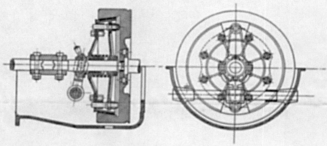

Sketch of Clutch.

PUMP. The water-circulating pump is fixed in a very convenient position on the side of the engine, and is gear-driven off the cam shaft.

FRAME. The frame is of stamped nickel steel.

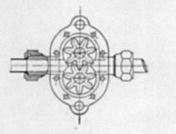

View of Pump.

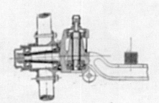

View of Front Axle.

SPRINGS. We have entirely remodelled the suspension of the car, and have confidence in asserting that it will be found as good as any on the market.

View of Four-Cylinder Engine.

View of Four-Cylinder Chassis.

SPECIFICATION OF
30-40 h.p. FOUR CYLINDER CHASSIS

CHASSIS ...	...	Wheelbase ... ... 10ft. 2in.
		Track ... ... 4ft. 6in.
		Road Wheels, artillery wheels, fitted with 920 × 120 m/m Pneumatic Tyres.
MOTOR ...	...	Number of Cylinders ... ... Four
		Bore ... ... 136 m/m.
		Stroke ... ... 150 m/m.
		Normal revolutions per minute 1000
IGNITION ...	...	High Tension Magneto, and Synchronised Electric Ignition with accumulator.
CARBURETTER ...		Our own special type of Automatic Carburetter.
LUBRICATION ...		Forced by pump driven by the Motor.
TRANSMISSION AND GEARING		Patent Leather-faced Cone Clutch. Four forward speeds and reverse. The direct drive being on the third speed. A propeller shaft transmits the power from the gear box to the back axle by means of bevel gearing.

At normal engine speeds the gears are:

1st	...	10 miles per hour
2nd	...	20 ,, ,,
3rd	...	30 ,, ,,
4th	...	40 ,, ,,

All changes operated by one lever.

AXLES AND STEERING ...	...	The front axle is a steel forging of " I " section. The pivot heads being fitted with ball bearings.
		The steering is effected through a reduction gear and is self-adjusting.
BRAKES ...	...	Two independent brakes are fitted.
		Double-acting hinged strap at end of Cardan Shaft, operated by foot pedal.
		Internally expanding brakes, fitted in drums of back wheels, and operated by hand lever.
CONTROL ...	...	Control and ignition levers mounted on steering wheel ; also foot accelerator.
PETROL CAPACITY		The petrol tank has a capacity of 14 gallons.
WEIGHT ...	...	Total weight of Chassis, 21 cwt.
FITTINGS ...	...	For list of fittings supplied with Chassis, see page 10.
		For price of Chassis and complete Car, see page 10.

View of Six-Cylinder Engine.

View of Six-Cylinder Chassis.

SPECIFICATION OF
35-45 h.p. SIX CYLINDER CHASSIS

CHASSIS ...	...	Wheelbase ... ... 10ft. 10in.
		Track ... ... 4ft. 6in.
		Road Wheels, artillery pattern, fitted with 880 × 120 m/m Pneumatic Tyres.
MOTOR ...	...	Number of Cylinders ... ... Six
		Bore ... ... 110 m/m
		Stroke ... ... 120 m/m
		Normal revolutions per minute 1000
IGNITION ...	...	High Tension Magneto and Synchronised Electric Ignition with Accumulators.
CARBURETTER	...	Our own special type of Automatic Carburetter.
LUBRICATION	...	Forced by pump driven by the Motor.

TRANSMISSION AND GEARING ... Patent Leather-faced Cone Clutch. Four speeds forward and reverse, the direct drive being on third speed. A propeller shaft transmits the power from the gear box to the back axle by means of bevel gearing.

At normal engine speeds the gears are :

1st	...	11 miles per hour.		
2nd	...	22	,,	,,
3rd	...	33	,,	,,
4th	...	44	,,	,,

All changes operated by one lever.

AXLES AND STEERING ... The front axle is a steel forging of " I " section, the pivot heads being fitted with ball bearings.

The steering is effected through a reduction gear and is self-adjusting.

BRAKES ... Two independent brakes are fitted :

> Double-acting metal to metal hinged strap at end of Cardan Shaft, operated by foot pedal.
>
> Internally expanding brakes, fitted in drums of back wheels, operated by hand lever.

CONTROL ... Control and ignition levers mounted on steering wheel ; also foot accelerator.

PETROL CAPACITY The petrol tank has a capacity of 14 gallons.

WEIGHT ... Total weight of Chassis, 21 cwt.

FITTINGS ... For list of fittings supplied with Chassis, see page 10.
For price of Chassis and complete Car, see page 10.

PRICES.

Price of 30-40 h.p. Four-Cylinder Chassis, with Tyres £650

A complete set of Tools is supplied with the Chassis.

Price of Car, with Side Entrance, Body to seat Five - £750

This price includes the tools mentioned, and also the following—Two side lamps, one tail lamp, one horn, two inner tubes, jack, pump, and repair outfit.

Price of 35-45 h.p. Six-Cylinder Chassis, with Tyres - £800

A complete set of Tools is supplied with the Chassis.

Price of Car, with Side Entrance, Body to seat Five - £900

This price includes the tools mentioned, and also the following—Two side lamps, one tail lamp, one horn, two inner tubes, jack, pump, and repair outfit.

The Cars can be painted any colour to suit purchaser's taste.

They are upholstered and finished in first-class style, both as regards workmanship and material, the leather used being of the best quality.

EXTRAS.

Double Extension Cape Cart Hood		£25 0 0
Folding Wind Screen		£10 0 0
Acetylene Head Lamps	from	£15 0 0

Landaulette or Limousine Body from £100 upwards extra.

GUARANTEE.

WE GIVE THE USUAL MAKER'S GUARANTEE.

LIST OF AWARDS.

Bronze Medal - Automobile Club de France.
1000 Miles Trial - 1900.

2nd Prize in Class A Automobile Club, G. B. & I.
1000 Miles Trial - 1900.

Daily Mail Prize Automobile Club, G. B. & I.
1000 Miles Trial - 1900.

The two Orleans Cars entered in the Automobile Club's Reliability Trials (650 miles) at Glasgow, in 1901, **gained more marks** : : : : : : : than any two Cars. : : : : : : :

The Orleans Car was awarded a **GOLD MEDAL** in the Automobile Club's last 100 Miles Trial (1903). It also gained **284 marks more than any other Petrol Car** in the trial.

Silver Medal in Sections II. (Parts) - - 1903.

Gold Medal, Bombay, January - 1905.

Tourist Trophy, September - - 1905.

Two Orleans Cars started 8th and 9th, beating as a team all others except the winners, averaging 28·7 and 27·8 miles per : : : : hour for the whole distance of 210 miles : : : :

Gold Medal. Irish Trials - - 1906.

Appendix VI. Plans: Orleans Motor Works

1903 and 1914

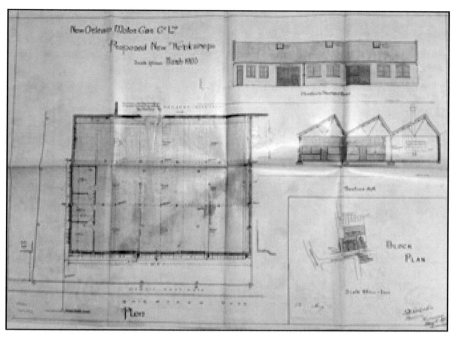

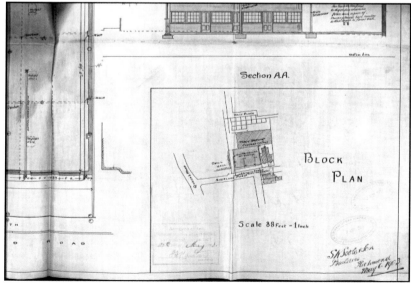

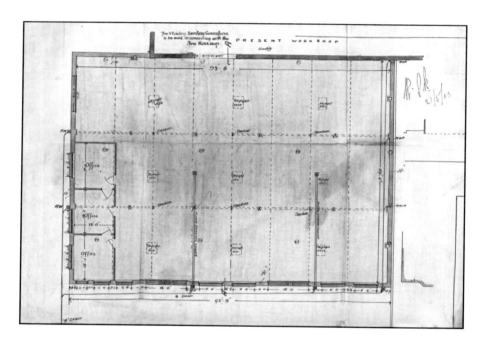

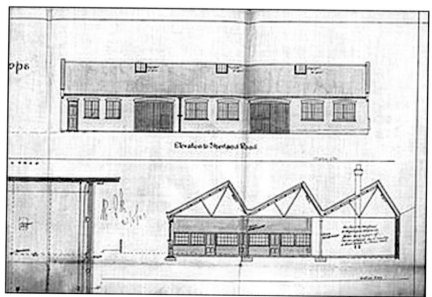

Elevation to Sherlaand Road

168

1914 Proposed Block Chimney by Straker-Squire Ltd.

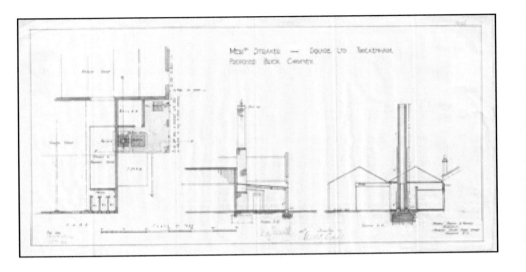

LIST OF FIGURES: MAPS, PHOTOGRAPHS

AND ILLUSTRATIONS

Figure numbers:

1   Cartoon of Twickenham's oldest surviving car, SX 13 drawn on an envelope addressed to Paul Edwards, owner of New Orleans Voiturette SX13. (*Courtesy of Paul Edwards*).

2   At a parade in Eastbourne, Simms' 1896 Daimler heralding the death knell of the horse-drawn age of road transport in Britain. (*Courtesy of Tom Clarke and the van Toll family*).

3   Map of Twickenham showing the location of Eel Pie Island and the motor works identified in this book.

4   Photograph of William Sargeant's boatyard and slipway on Eel Pie Island c1893. (*Courtesy of Tom Clarke and the van Toll family*).

5a/b/c   Extracts from the original contract (indenture) for the sale of the Eel Pie Island Boatyard by Andrew Pears and his family to Frederick Simms and the Daimler Motor Co. dated 18th August 1896. (*Courtesy of Eel Pie Island Museum*).

6   1900 "New Orleans" Voiturette advertisement. (*Courtesy of Grace's Guide*).

7   'New Orleans Voiturette' plate on the front of 8710 MN. (*Courtesy of Andrew Kelsey and the Milntown House Trust, IOM*).

8   The photograph shows van Toll at the wheel of a Voiturette. (*Courtesy of Tom Clarke and the van Toll family*).

9   Burford and van Toll advertisement that used the relief of Mafeking to promote their cars. (*Courtesy of Grace's Guide*).

10   An advertisement for the New Orleans using the success on the Automobile Club's Across Britain 1000 mile Trial to promote it. (*Courtesy of Grace's Guide*).

11a/b   Two photographs of New Orleans Voiturette 8710 MN formerly AX 21, showing:
a. The air-cooled transverse twin-cylinder engine is made from two one-cylinder engines joined by the flywheel.
b. The driver's basic controls on a 1900 Voiturette.
(*Courtesy of Andrew Kelsey and the Milntown House Trust, IOM*).

170

12a/b   Ching & Co. '*Veteran and Vintage Cars*' cigarette card No.4 New Orleans (1900). *(source: internet auction site)*

13   An advertisement for the Automobile Club's 1899 Richmond Car Show. *(Courtesy of Grace's Guide).*

14   A Lanchester on Petersham Hill, Richmond during the hill climbing test in June 1899. *(Courtesy of Grace's Guide).*

15   A 1904 15 hp New Orleans. *(Courtesy of David Hales).*

16   Tim Summers' 1901 3.5 hp single-cylinder car, BS 8654 at Brighton having completed the Veteran car run in November 2019.

17   Goad Fire Insurance map (1907) of central Twickenham. *(Courtesy of Richmond Local Studies Centre: Reference number LM/1141).*

18   Extract from an oblique aerial photograph of central Twickenham looking north, with the Cross Deep junction with King Street before it was widened in the foreground c1925. *(Courtesy of Richmond Local Studies Centre: Reference number LCF/4932 in aerial photos box L 526.982 oversize).*

19   The 1905 Certificate of Performance for the 15hp Orleans car at the TT Race on the Isle of Man, 14th September 1905. *(Courtesy of Richmond Local Studies Centre: Mott Collection Box 3).*

20   Advertisement for the 15 hp Orleans car, February 1905. *(Courtesy of Grace's Guide).*

21   Photograph of a 15 hp Orleans car c1905/6. *(Courtesy of David Hales and John Warburton).*

22   The Orleans Four-Cylinder Chassis, with tyres and the 30-40 hp engine, November 1907. (*source: 1907 Orleans brochure*).

23   Dr. Langdon Down's 1905 35 hp Orleans limousine. *(Courtesy of David Hales and the Langdon Down family).*

24   FX 344 was exhibited by Orleans Cars at the 1907 Olympia Motor Show. (*Courtesy of David Hales and the Langdon Down family).*

25   From the back page of 1907 Ford catalogue. *(source: Perry, Thornton & Schreiber's catalogue: Ford cars 1907).*

26   Ford Model Ns under construction using mass-production methods. *(source: Perry, Thornton & Schreiber's catalogue: Ford cars 1907).*

27   Map showing the 'Works' on the corner of Orleans and Chapel Roads.

28   1896 photograph of King Street on *'the day the circus came to town'*. The Orleans Cycle Works is on the far right of the photograph. *(Courtesy of Richmond Local Studies Centre: Reference number: LCF/18309).*

29   Advertisement in the *Richmond Herald 18th June 1898. (Source: The Richmond Herald).*

30   Photograph of the rear of No.12 King Street advertising *'Motor, Cycle & General engineers'* and *'Motor Experts'* with *'C. Heal'*, the blacksmith next door in Pound Lane c1900. *(Courtesy of Richmond Local Studies Centre and BOTLHS paper 'Twickenham though a chemist's window 1914-1929').*

31   Photograph of Tamplin's Garage with Cecil Tamplin standing outside, 20-22 Heath Road Twickenham. *(Courtesy of Howard Webb).*

32a/b   Two photographs of the *'Works'* on the corner of Orleans and Chapel Road taken by the author in 2018.

33   Photograph c1900 of John van Toll and his wife Florence with their two sons, Thomas and John. *(Courtesy of Tom Clarke and the Van Toll family).*

34   The photograph shows Evelyn Ellis at the wheel of his Panhard-Levessor at a motor show held at Tunbridge Wells on 15th October 1895. *(Courtesy of Tom Clarke and Michael Jeal).*

35   Photograph of Van Toll driving the Daimler Landau *Modern Times* on the *'Emancipation Run'* on which Gottlieb Daimler, Wilhelm Maybach and Frederick Simms were passengers. *(Courtesy of Tom Clarke and Michael Jeal).*

36a   Van Toll, Mayer & Co., Motor Engineers. Their motorcar depot and garage at 91-93 Richmond Road, Twickenham c1900's. *(Courtesy of Howard Webb).*

36b   The same view over 110 years later. *(Courtesy of Graham Stanley).*

37   *'Van Toll, Mayer & Co., Motor Engineers'*. Motor and Marine Engineers. *(Courtesy of Howard Webb).*

38   Orleans Garage photographed by the author in 2018.

39   1909 advertisement for *'Erade and Van Toll'* in Twickenham shows the renewed association with the Belgian motor manufacturer, Vivinus. *(Courtesy of Tom Clarke and the van Toll family).*

40   Photograph of *'John'* van Toll's headstone. Buried with his son *'Boynie"* and wife Florence at Twickenham Cemetery. *(Courtesy of Graham Stanley).*

41 February 1905 advertisements for Beaufort's exhibits at the Olympia Motor Exhibition. *(Courtesy of Grace's Guide).*

42 Map showing the location of the Beaufort Engineering Works on the site of the Roseneath Stables, adjoining Marble Hill Park.

43 The Beaufort 24-32 hp chain driven omnibus chassis. *(source: Commercial Motor 23rd November 1905, reference kindly provided by Roger Wyer).*

44 Goad Fire Insurance map (1907) extract: Strawberry Vale, Twickenham. *(Courtesy of Richmond Local Studies Centre).*

45 Goad Fire Insurance map (1907) extract: Twickenham Road and Manor Road, Teddington. *(Courtesy of Richmond Local Studies Centre).*

46 A photograph of a Scott, Stirling Pioneer bus seen at the Olympia Motor Exhibition in 1905. *(source: Commercial Motor 23rd November 1905, reference kindly provided by Roger Wyer).*

47 A Scott, Stirling double-decker en route to Cricklewood. *(source: The Automobile June 1906, reference kindly provided by Roger Wyer).*

48 A Scott, Stirling single-decker at the Rosapenna Hotel in Donegal. *(source Robert Welch, Ireland's Eye 1905, reference kindly provided by Roger Wyer).*

49 The map shows the substantial building on the corner of Richmond Road and Oak Lane, marked *'Carriage Factory'.*

50 A photograph of the Corben Carriage Factory built in 1852. *(Courtesy of Richmond Local Studies Centre: Reference number LCF/21176).*

51 The 1905 Corben built GWR *'observation car'*, a charabanc seating 16 passengers with luggage carried on the roof. *(source: Commercial Motor' 21 September 1905, reference kindly provided by Roger Wyer).*

52 Goad Fire Insurance map (1907) extract: Corben Brothers 'Carriage and Motor Car Factory'. *(Courtesy of Richmond Local Studies Centre).*

53 The photograph/postcard with sign that reads *'Coachwork by the Twickenham Motor Co. Ltd. Twickenham'. (Courtesy of Kenneth Lea, Twickenham & Teddington Histories Facebook page).*

54 The Lyric Palace with Twickenham Motor Company next door. The photograph shows two cars of the period that can be seen outside, and a sign offering *'Cars for Hire'. (Courtesy of Cinema Theatre Association Archive).*

55   From the same period, the aerial photograph shows the Lyric Palace Cinema (centre) and the distinctive garage building next door on the corner of Oak Lane. *(Courtesy of Cinema Theatre Association Archive).*

56   Dating from November 1913, an advertisement for the 10 hp Wyvern Light Car. *(Courtesy of Grace's Guide).*

57   A 1914 advertisement for Twickenham Motor Co. Ltd. *(Courtesy of Grace's Guide).*

58   A photograph of an Autovan commercial vehicle of the period. *(Courtesy of Craig Horner and The Automobile magazine).*

59   Photograph of 9-11, Richmond Road c1925, by then A.W.Bradbury & Co.Ltd. *(source: Richmond Guardian, reference kindly provided by Roger Wyer).*

60   Photograph showing the result of a huge storm that struck Twickenham one night in August 1926 destroying Bradbury's Garage. *(source: Roger Annett, Twickenham & Teddington Histories Facebook page).*

61   Photograph of Spikins Garage in January 1968. The roof of the old Lyric Palace cinema can be seen behind. *(Courtesy of Mike Cherry).*

62   Map showing the Engineering Works in Gould Road near Twickenham Green where Medina Engineering Co made Mercury cars.

63   November 1919 advertisement, showing a Mercury car at the end of May Road. Twickenham Green and Holy Trinity Church are in the background. *(Courtesy of Grace's Guide).*

64   The photograph shows a 10 hp 2-seater Mercury car of 1919. *(Courtesy of Andrew Minney).*

65   WH Arnold & Co advertisement for the 'Eclipse' All-weather Body. *(Courtesy of Coachbuild)*

66   Mercury Cars bonnet mascot depicting the Roman god Mercury 'The Messenger'. *(source: Mercury Cars 1920 Catalogue).*

67   Photograph of the first experimental two-seater car Taunton built in Twickenham in 1912. *(Courtesy of Michael Worthington-Williams and The Automobile magazine).*

68   Photograph of the prototype standard four-seater Taunton 14hp model. *(Courtesy of Michael Worthington-Williams and The Automobile magazine).*

69   Photograph of the 1912 Taunton engine... a 14.4 hp overhead-inlet, side-exhaust, single casting. *(Courtesy of Michael Worthington-Williams and The Automobile magazine).*

70   The cover for the 1914 Taunton brochure, produced in advance of it's anticipated launch. *(Courtesy of Michael Worthington-Williams and The Automobile magazine).*

71   The 1920 Lington's *'For the Light Car Connoisseur'* advertisement, gives 61 London Road, Twickenham as the company's address. *(Courtesy of Grace's Guide).*

72a/b 61, London Road, already with an engineering business in the photograph and a detail of the shop. *(Courtesy of Howard Webb).*

73   February 1914 advertisement for Straker-Squire's 'World's Best' cars. *(Courtesy of Grace's Guide).*

74   An advertisement for the Straker-Squire truck showing the works location in Sherland Road, Twickenham in *The Motor Trader,* 12th April 1916. *(Courtesy of Grace's Guide).*

75a   The kneeling Spirit of Ecstasy used on the Rolls Royce Phantom IV. *(Courtesy of Heritage Auctions, HA.com)*

75b   Straker-Squire kneeling nickel plated radiator mascot, side view. *(Courtesy of Grace's Guide).*

75c   Driver's view of the radiator mascot. *(Courtesy of Grace's Guide).*

76   Photograph of one of two surviving Straker-Squire 6-cylinder cars with the characteristic radiator mascot. *(Courtesy of Grace's Guide).*

77   Written on the back of this photograph, dated February 1917... *'Munitions Workers, Straker-Squire, Sherland Road, Twickenham'.* *(Courtesy of Howard Webb).*

78a/b/c Recent photographs taken by the author of the Orleans Works site, now a car park, showing the two original gateways into the site from Sherland Road.

79   Advertisement for the 1909 Berliet model on offer through their London agents. *(Courtesy of Grace's Guide).*

80   Map showing the location of the Berliet Motor works in Cambridge Road adjacent to the old skating rink.

81   A 1930 advertisement for the range of Berliet trucks with the Cambridge Road address. *(Courtesy of Grace's Guide).*

82   Photograph of a Berliet bus offered for sale in 1927. *(source: Commercial Motor 18th January 1927, reference kindly provided by Roger Wyer).*

83   Map showing the location of the Winchester Works in Winchester Road, St Margarets. The area was cleared to construct the A316 Chertsey Road c1930 and the factory demolished. The Art Deco *'Globe Central'* factory was built on the Winchester Works site alongside the A316.

84   Photograph of a Grigg motor scooter from 1928 in the Hull Streetlife Museum. *(Courtesy of Grace's Guide).*

85   August 1923 advertisement for a Grigg motorcycle and sidecar. *(Courtesy of Grace's Guide).*

86   1919 advertisement for Wooler motorcycles. *(Courtesy of Grace's Guide).*

87   Cartoon drawn of the W G C Hayward's Whippet ... *'runs like a big six'.* *(Courtesy of Andy Bufton and The British Motorcycle Charitable Trust).*

88   Photograph of the restored Whippet scooter at the Sammy Miller Museum for the British Motorcycle Charitable Trust. *(Courtesy of Andy Bufton and The British Motorcycle Charitable Trust.*

89   Advertisement claiming that the Argson was the *'World's best tricycle'* was aimed at those that had lost a limb in the First World War. *(source: online auction website, reference kindly provided by Roger Wyer).*

90   Photograph of Argson NPF 224, seen at classic car show. *(Courtesy of Graces Guide).*

91   The Motor Cycle magazine article about the P&P experimental compact two-stroke. *(source: The Motorcycle 20th April 1922).*

92   Photograph of a 1914 Carden Monocar car with John Carden at the wheel. *(Courtesy of Grace's Guide).*

93   A 1916 advertisement for the Carden' Monocar with the Somerset Road address in Teddington. *(Courtesy of Grace's Guide).*

94   The photograph shows a Monocar being manually lowered from the upper floor of the premises in Somerset Road. *(Courtesy of Andrew Minney).*

95   The map shows the location of the Somerset Road works, close to the junction with Church Road.

96   The March 1919 advertisement for the AV two-seater *'Bi-Car'.* *(Courtesy of Grace's Guide).*

97   The photograph shows the Church Road side of the site while the Monocar was in production. *(Courtesy of Andrew Minney).*

98   The back wall of the building on the right of the photograph is all that remains of the works today. *(Courtesy of Andrew Minney).*

99   NH 3610 owned by Gerry Michelmore, is seen in the photograph. (Courtesy of Roger Armstrong).

100   The Aston Martin logo.

101   Map showing the Monarch *'Motor Works'* site. The Boathouse was close to the area marked *'Wharf'* on the map.

102   Photograph of the *'Monarch Motor Launches'* made by Monarch Motor Co Ltd seen moored on the riverbank at Teddington. *(Courtesy of Grace's Guide).*

103a   Photograph of the Monarch boathouse and workshop with a Monarch Motor launch moored on the adjacent riverbank. (*Courtesy of Dr Helen Baker*).

103b   Photograph of the boathouse with the addition of a sympathetic restaurant kitchen extension taken by the author in March 2020.

104a   Photograph of the old boathouse, now a restaurant (The Wharf) with a large enclosed verandah, seen from the other side of the river at Teddington Lock. Photograph taken by the author in 2020.

104b   The boathouse looking much as it would have as Monarch Motor Launches boathouse. Photograph taken by the author in 2020.

105   Map of the location of the British Anzani motor works in Hampton Hill.

106   A photograph taken in 1948 of the British Anzani works entrance in Windmill Road. *(Courtesy of British Anzani Archive).*

107   British Anzani *Iron Horse* advertisement. (*Courtesy of Grace's Guide).*

108   Photograph of a restored *Iron Horse* being demonstrated. (*Courtesy of Grace's Guide).*

109   An advertisement for the Anzani's *'leading range'* of outboard motors, giving the Windmill Road address. (*Courtesy of Grace's Guide).*

110   Advertisement for the *'Astra Commercial Car'*. *(Courtesy of British Anzani Archive).*

111   Photograph of the Astra Utility light car and delivery van. (*Courtesy of Lane Motor Museum, Nashville, Tennessee, USA).*

112a/b/c Photographs of 192 XUM showing the rather basic nature of the Astra Utility. (*Courtesy of Lane Motor Museum, Nashville, Tennessee, USA).*

113   1912 advertisement for the *'AC Sociable'* giving the Thames Ditton address. *(Courtesy of Grace's Guide).*

114 An aerial photograph of Taggs Island, the hotel and tennis courts before the bridge was built to connect the Island to the Hampton mainland. (*Courtesy of John Sheaf*).

115 Photograph of the AC Model 70/AC 70 built for the Ministry of Pensions. (*Courtesy of Britain by Car*).

116 Photograph/postcard of one of Southend Pier's four seven-carriage trains built on Tagg's Island. (*Courtesy of Tony Thorpe and Dixie Diesel*).

117 Photograph of AC70 RRF19R at the Lakeland Motor Museum. (*Courtesy of Grace's Guide*).

118 Photograph of W. F. Tamplin, Cycle Makers shop at No.4 Staines Road Terrace, Twickenham Green. (*source: Tamplin family, Twickenham and Teddington Histories Facebook page*).

118a WF Tamplin business card. (*source: Tamplin family, courtesy of Mike Thurston*).

119 Advertisement with photographs of the shop and the cycle Works, at 12 King Street. (*source: online family history website, reference kindly provided by Roger Wyer*).

120 Photograph of W. F. Tamplin, King Street premises, offering, '*Motor & Cycle repairs*' at street level with the first floor used as the cycle works. (*source: Tamplin family, courtesy of Mike Thurston*).

121a/b Photograph of King Street showing Tamplin's showrooms at No.12 on the far right of the photo, selling Wolseley cars, amongst others and a detail from the photograph. (*Courtesy of Richmond Local Studies Centre: Reference number: LCF/2523*).

122 Sketch map entitled '*Proposed Stopping-up of Pound Lane*' dated July 1931. (*Courtesy of Richmond Local Studies Centre: Reference number: LM/3183*).

123 Photograph of the Tamplin & Pangbourne car showroom on the corner of York Road and Church Street in Twickenham. (*Courtesy of Alan Winter*).

124a/b Photograph of Tamplin's Servicing and Repairs depot opposite the Old Station Yard at No.2 Queens Road and a detail from the photograph. (*Courtesy of Richmond Local Studies Centre: Reference number: LCF/15733*).

125 Photograph of the former Tamplin's repair depot taken in 2021 by the author.

126 Photograph taken in 1908 of George Kingsbury and Son. Cycle Manufacturers, at 3, Red Lion Square, Hampton. (*Courtesy of John Sheaf*).

127 Photograph of George Kingsbury at the wheel of his first car, a Humber 10/12, in 1905. (*Courtesy of John Sheaf*).

128 Photograph of CA Blay's first premises, at No.2 Briar Road just off the Green, c1912. (*Courtesy of Bob Anderson*).

129 Photograph c1930 of CA Blay's premises at 192, Heath Road with Charles Blay, his daughter Anne and Jim Gilkes, who she later married. (*Courtesy of Bob Anderson*).

130 Advertisement from the 1930s, when Blay's were selling three-wheeler cars, as well as cycles and motorcycles. (*source: The Richmond Cinema, Sept 1932, reference kindly provided by Roger Wyer*).

131 Photograph of motorcycle enthusiast Ken Blay, racing a motorcycle and sidecar. (*Courtesy of Bob Anderson*).

132 Photograph of James Palmer outside the shop with a range of his bikes. (*Courtesy of Chris French, Joy and Claire Palmer*)

133 Photograph of the Mid-Surrey Cycling Club. (*Courtesy of Joy and Claire Palmer*).

134 Photograph of the petrol pumps on the pavement outside 109 Stanley Road. (*Courtesy of Chris French*).

135 Photograph of Palmers showrooms at Nos 119 and 121, a few doors away from No.109. (*Courtesy of Chris French, Joy and Claire Palmer*).

136 Advertisement for Palmer's as an agent and distributers for Lambretta motor scooters. (*source: The Motor Cycle June 1958, reference kindly provided by Roger Wyer*).

137 Photograph of David Palmer outside the showroom in Stanley Road with his grass-track bike. (*Courtesy of Chris French*).

138 Mercury Engineering Company letter heading. (*Courtesy of the Rees family*).

139 Map showing the location of Mercury Engineering Co. in Strawberry Vale with Swan Island behind. The location of the Racing Services Partnership workshop and the 'Milham's Motor & Boat Building Works' is also shown.

140 A photograph taken in 1929 showing a car being served with petrol at the Strawberry Vale site before it became Mercury Engineering Co. (*Courtesy of the Rees family*).

141 This 1940s wartime shot of Mercury, shows a car with white-painted mudguards, black-out headlamps and gas bag on the car roof. *(Courtesy of the Rees family)*.

142 Photograph of the 1950s built car showroom and spares department in addition to the car servicing and repairs workshop. *(Courtesy of the Rees family)*.

143 Photograph of Mercury Motors first pick-up truck, a Ford E83W. Anthony really wishes that they'd kept it! *(Courtesy of the Rees family)*.

144 Map showing the location of the extensive Automotive Engineering Co. works between Twickenham Green and Colne Road.

145 Advertisement for BHB '*Self-adjusting pistons*' made by Automotive Engineering. *(Courtesy of Grace's Guide)*

146 Map showing the location of 156, Amyand Park Road and Crown Yard off Crown Road. Also 148, Amyand Park Road and the Emeryson Car Works.

147 Map of the '*Motor Works*' at the Arlington Works in St Margarets c1935.

148 1930's aerial photograph the Wilson Motor Body Building Co. offering '*A Body For Every Trade*'. (*source: Twickenham Park Residents Association*).

149 Photograph taken by the author of the long corrugated-iron clad shed still in use in 2020, a little the worse for wear.

150 Harford Baby Cars Ltd., Arlington Works advertised in the Daily Mirror Saturday 22nd November 1924. *(source: Daily Mirror, Saturday 22nd November 1924)*.

151 1940s photograph of P & S Motors site in Waldegrave Road where they sold petrol as well as Bedford commercial vehicles. *(Courtesy of Richmond Local Studies Centre: Reference number: LCF/16941)*.

152 Photographs taken by the author in 1964 of a fire that broke out at Palmer Coachbuilder's Waldegrave Road works.

153 1965 advertisement for Palmer in *The Commercial Motor*. (*source: Commercial Motor April 1965, reference kindly provided by Roger Wyer*)

154 Photograph taken as Paul Emery (No.28) overtakes Jack Leary (No.21) on a bend at Brands Hatch in April 1951 race where Bernie Ecclestone gained 4th place in the final. *(Courtesy of 500 race org)*.

155 Emeryson specification sheet. *(Courtesy of 500 race org)*.

156 Photograph of the Emeryson Formula 3 500-8 outside the Emeryson Cars workshop c1950/51. *(Courtesy of the Duncan Rabagliati collection)*.

157 Photograph taken by the author of the Emeryson works site in Amyand Park Road still with a motoring connection in 2020.

158 Photograph of Paul Emery driving a F1 Emeryson-Alta. *(Courtesy of the Duncan Rabagliati collection).*

159 Photograph of the last surviving 1961 Emeryson-Climax Formula 1 racing car sold at Bonhams in 2017 for £161,000. *(Courtesy of Bonhams, reference kindly provided by Mike Cherry).*

160 Photograph taken in the 1930s of The Bantam outside Spikins in Heath Road, Twickenham. *(Courtesy of Neil Thorp and the Spikins family... from an album owned by Robert Spikins).*

161a/b Spikins advertisement in the *Autocar,* 10th April 1936 and a detail from the advertisement. *(Courtesy of Neil Thorp).*

162 Photograph of the Cromard Special - being driven by Ken Wharton. *(Courtesy of the Wolverhampton History and Heritage Society).*

163 Spikins Garage... petrol station and local agent for a wide range of British marques, selling and servicing cars, as the advertisement shows. *(Courtesy of Andrew Minney).*

164 The *'Race Proved by Willments'* logo.

165 Photograph of John Willment behind the wheel of an early prototype inside the motor racing workshop that he built behind Willments Garage. *(Courtesy of 500race.org).*

166 The photograph taken at the *Formule Libre* race at the 1957 Brands Hatch, Boxing Day meeting shows a Willment sports/racing car on the front row of the grid with Stuart Lewis-Evans driving. *(Courtesy of the Duncan Rabagliati collection).*

167 Photograph of the Willment-Climax LSL 893 of 1959. *(Courtesy of Michael Marsh).*

168 Definitely an inspiration for the 1960's Batmobile! *(Courtesy of coachbuild.com).*

169 Map showing the location of Biggs, Walter James Coach builders, later to become Obey's Garage No.113 Heath Road. The workshops built behind were used by Willments, Bracey-Price and David Price Racing in the latter part of the 20th century.

170 Photograph of the site (taken by the author in 2022) which now hosts the MKG3000 car dealership. The former workshops are now MKG's car service bays.

171 Milham's boathouse on Swan Island in a photograph taken between 1905 and 1914. *(Courtesy of Mike Cherry).*

172a/b Photograph of Heath Road in 1904 showing the carriage works in the distance on the right hand side and a detail from the photograph. *(Courtesy of Richmond Local Studies centre: Reference number LCF/2930).*

173 Photograph of Racing Services engineering workshop with John Miles, former Formula 1 racing driver for Lotus and BRM working on an engine. *(source: Motor Sport magazine).*

174 Robert Bamford, seen in the photograph, was the engineering genius behind the Bamford and Martin motoring partnership. *(Courtesy of John Paul Jacques).*

175 Racing Services (Engines) Ltd. and their logo.

176 Photograph of a toolbox from Racing Services days at their former workshop taken by the author in 2020.

177a/b The light-weight tubular steel space frames which were attached to the front and rear of the wooden monocoque, as the photographs show. *(Courtesy of Roger Nathan).*

178 Photograph of a Costin-Nathan GT at the Motor Show with the *'Powered by Rootes'* slogan on the door. *(Courtesy of Roger Nathan).*

179 The Costin-Nathan won every national and international event in which it was entered between 1966 and 1970. *(Courtesy of Roger Nathan).*

180 Photograph of the prototype Costin-Nathan restored by Roger Nathan, now on indefinite loan to the National Motor Museum at Beaulieu. *(Courtesy of Roger Nathan).*

181 Photograph of Henry Cornelius Hunter taken in the 1930s. *(Courtesy of the Hunter family).*

182 Map of Twickenham showing Eel Pie Island and the location of 8 Sion Road. Sargeant's extensive boatyard, workshops and slipway can be seen on the map c1898.

183 1911 census with Henry recorded as a *Motor and Marine engineer*.

184a/b/c A photograph of the wooden *'margarine box'* containing three brown paper bags full of motoring literature dating from the 1900s; a selection of motor manufacturers brochures and catalogues; brochures, leaflets and letters from suppliers of a range of motor vehicle parts. *(The author's photographs).*

185 A letter dated 21st November 1910 to Van Toll & Co. Ltd. from The Aster Engineering Company. *(Courtesy of the Hunter family).*

186 View of Orleans Road looking north c1920 with the site of Henry's garages on the west side of the road. *(Courtesy of Richmond Local Studies: Centre Vertical file – Orleans Road, Twickenham – Newspaper Cuttings and Photographs).*

187 Lock-up garages still run along the west side of Orleans Road in this 2018 photograph taken by the author.

188 Triumph Motor Cycles *Preliminary Motor Catalogue for 1907* as their full catalogue was not yet ready. *(Courtesy of the Hunter family).*

189 Triumph Cycle Company's letter to Henry, offering him a motor trade discount of 10% and another 2.5% off for cash on a new motorcycle. *(Courtesy of the Hunter family).*

190 Photograph of Henry, Rosa and their daughter Ruby outside No. 8 Sion Road in 1916. *(Courtesy of the Hunter family).*

191 Photograph of Roberta Cowell at the wheel of an Emeryson racing car at the Shelsley Walsh hill climb in September 1957. *(Kind permission of Mary Evans Picture Library © Illustrated London News Ltd).*

192 An extract from the *'Commemoration Run List of Entrants'* for 4th November 1956 showing four New Orleans cars participating. *(Courtesy of Brooklands Motor Museum Library).*

193 Photograph of New Orleans Voiturette, AX 74 in the 1950's. *(Courtesy of Andrew Kelsey/Milntown House Trust Collection).*

194 Photograph of AX 74 which was later reregistered 8710 MN on the Isle of Man. *(Courtesy of Andrew Kelsey/Milntown House Trust Collection).*

195 Photograph of Paul Edwards diving SX 13 across the finishing line at Madeira Drive in Brighton at the end of the 2019 London to Brighton Veteran Car Run. *(Courtesy of Paul Edwards).*

196 Newspaper article featuring *Voiturette* EW 113 with Mrs Elsie Van Toll at the wheel, Johannes's daughter-in-law from the *Surrey Comet* May 1981. *(Courtesy of Twickenham Museum: Dick Cashmore archive).*

197 Receipt showing that Alan Edwards bought SX 13 from JH White for the sum of £35 in 1953. *(Courtesy of Paul Edwards).*

198 Photograph of Paul and his father crossing Westminster Bridge in SX 13 in 2000, marking the car's 100th anniversary. *(Courtesy of Paul Edwards).*

199 Photograph of Paul driving SX 13 along Marine Drive in Brighton at the end of the London to Brighton Run with his wife Jo and son Tom. *(Courtesy of Paul Edwards)*.

200 2016 photograph of Tom at the wheel... the next generation to love SX 13. *(Courtesy of Paul Edwards)*.

201 The brass plaque attached to the front of the car reads... *'To live in the hearts you leave behind is not to die'. (Courtesy of Paul Edwards)*.

202 Photograph of AX 74 on Madeira Drive in Brighton. It must have been a welcome sight after a 62 mile journey on a wet November day in a vehicle that lacks even the most rudimentary weather protection. *(Courtesy of Andrew Kelsey and the Milntown House Trust Collection)*.

203 Photograph of Bob Thomas driving on with the broken crankshaft. Sir Clive follows In a Lea Francis "woody" and a trailer.*(Courtesy of Andrew Kelsey and the Milntown House Trust Collection)*.

204 Photograph showing that the Voiturette's lighting is by candles in spring loaded holders. *(Courtesy of Andrew Kelseyand and the Milntown House Trust Collection)*.

205 A pen and ink sketch by a friend of Paul Edwards of his 1900 Voiturette, SX 13. *(Courtesy of Paul Edwards)*.

Appendix IV.

New Orleans Handbook and Specifications 1900. *(Courtesy of Jonathan Rishton, The Automobile Magazine)*.

Appendix V.

The Orleans Motor Co. Ltd. Catalogue c1907. *(Courtesy of the Hunter family)*.

Appendix VI.

Plans: Orleans Motor Works 1903 and 1914. *(Courtesy of Richmond Local Studies Centre: Reference number: PLA/09187 and PLA/09188)*.

Please note that every effort has been made to contact the owners or copyright holders of all the illustrations used in this local history paper. The publishers will be pleased to amend in future editions any errors or omissions brought to their attention.

REFERENCES

1. Widely used and quoted: Frederick Simms exhibition at the Museum of London and the *'Open Plaques'* blue plaque to Frederick Simms in Fulham.

2. *'Lawson's Bicyclette'* 1879.

3. *Grace's Guide to British Industrial History.* UK Manufacturers: Road Vehicles: Motorcycles: Pre-WWI.

4. *Autocar* magazine 3rd February 1900.

5. Graham Stanley's correspondence with Rob Hilliard, great grandson of W.H.Astell.

6. *'Gigmanity'* was Thomas Carlisle's satirical symbol of middle-class respectability. *'One that keeps a* gig' (an open horse-drawn owner-driven carriage). *Autocar* magazine 3rd February 1900.

7. *Automotor* magazine 1906 quoted in *The Automobile* magazine article May 1995 'The New Orleans... fact or fiction?' by David Hales.

8. *Grace's Guide to British Industrial History.*

9. *Daily Telegraph & Courier* (London) 18th November 1908.

10. *The Car* magazine 'A Good Six-cylinder' 20th February 1907.

11. *The Motor-Car Journal* 'The New Orleans Motor-Voiturette' 19th January 1900.

12. Letter from Edward Tamplin to Clive Edwards about the Voiturette dated February 1946. From an archive at Miltown House 'Thomas Collection' of historic vehicles.

13. *Kelly's Directory* (or *Kelly's, Post Office and Harrod & Co Directory*) a trade directory that listed all businesses and tradespeople in a town. Richmond 1900/01 edition.

14. The National Archives: New Orleans Motor Co. Ltd. Registration document 22nd March 1901.

15. *Middlesex Independent* 2nd November 1901. Report of the H.M Inspectorate of Factories prosecution for a breach of the Factories Act.

16. Borough of Twickenham planning application dated May 1903.

17. 'The first motor-car journey in England: a driving controversy' by Tom Clarke 2016-18.

18. 'The Lawson Era' by David Burgess-Wise.

19. Lloyd's List 25th November 1909.

20. *The Daily Telegraph & Courier* 12th December 1905.

21. *Commercial Motor* 23rd November 1905.

22. *The Sporting Times* Saturday 24 October 1908.

23. *Coventry Evening Telegraph* 17th March 1915.

24. Interestingly the highly decorated interior barrel-roof of the cinema has survived above the false ceiling of the premises today, sadly hidden out of sight (EPIM team).

25. *The Automobile* magazine 'Ahead of its time' by Michael Worthington-Williams April 1989.

26. *Globe* newspaper March 1915.

27. The National Archives: Plan of Ministry of Munitions.

28. *Commercial Motor* 18th January 1927.

29. *Old Bike* magazine David Earnshaw Autumn edition 1995.

30. 'Grigg...' by Martyn Day St. Margarets Community 28th August 2015.

31. *The Motor Cycle* magazine.

32. *Motor Sport* magazine 'Cyclecar Capers' July 1995.

33. *Richmond and Twickenham Times* 4th Dec. 2008.

34. email from Spencer Silverbach American Bentley enthusiast quoting from WO Bentley's autobiography, 'My Life and My Cars and Bentley Factory Cars 1919 - 1931'.

35. *Kelly's Directory*: various years.

36. Angie Boon's research on J. C. Wilson in the Electoral Register (Twickenham and Teddington History Facebook page, 10th March 2022).

37. *Motor Sport* magazine 'The Cars of Paul Emery' March 1985.

38. '*The History of the Spikins Hudson Special*' by Neil Thorp 2014 and emails to the author in August 2023.

39. *Motor Sport* magazine 'Willment-Past and Present' June 1966.

40. '1964 Willment Daytona Coupe CSX2131' Shelby American Collection Museum.

41. *Motor Sport* magazine 'Bites as good as it barks' article November 2003.

42. 'When a MotoGP legend joined an F1 race at Imola' by Sam Smith the-race.com 1st November 2020.

43. David Price quoted in the-race.com 1st November 2020.

44. *Motor Sport* magazine 'Racing Services' September 1976.

45. *Motor Sport* magazine 'Innovation and Escape' April 2016.

46. *Octane* magazine August issue 2019.

47. Roger Nathan's emails to the author.

48. 'Richmond and Twickenham Home Journal' Parish Magazine Nov. 1917.

49. *Roberta Cowell's Story* by Roberta Cowell (Heinemann) 1954.

50. The British Newspaper Archive Blog: 'The Most Talked Of Woman In England'.

51. Conversations between the author and Dave Alderson in 2019 before he retired and Alderson's Garage closed for good.

52. David Hales research into registration numbers and the New Orleans cars.

ACKNOWLEDGEMENTS

I MUST FIRST THANK those at Eel Pie Island Museum: museum curator Michele Whitby for setting me off on my journey, Celia Holman for her help and enthusiasm and (the late) Clive Burton for his extensive knowledge and research into Eel Pie Island's boatyard. Janine Stanford and her team at Richmond Local Studies Centre for pointing me towards my first Twickenham cars. Mike Cherry, editor on behalf of the Borough of Twickenham Local History Society, for his encouragement, patience and for sharing the late Dick Cashmore's motoring archive with me at Twickenham Museum. Thanks too, for putting me in touch with local historian Dr Helen Baker and her research into the Tough-Brothers site in Teddington, and local researcher Graham Stanley. Particular thanks to Graham for sharing all his research into the Orleans Motor Works, his contact with William Astall's family and his help at The National Archives. Also to Brooklands Museum, for the use of their library and archives. Huge thanks to local historian Roger Wyer for discovering some of the more obscure Twickenham cars by sifting through numerous newspaper archives. Thanks also to John Sheaf for his research into Kingsbury's in Hampton, and to Nick Kingsbury. Also to Alan Frost at Orleans Garage and Michael Webster for introducing me to Bob Anderson, former managing director of Blay's motorcycles, for all his help, knowledge, photographs and stories about Blay's. Thanks to Barry Gillon at MKG for putting me in touch with Dave Morley former Service Manager for his help with cars built at the Obey's Garage site. Similarly to David Palmer's wife Joy and daughter Claire for all their help, stories and photographs of the Palmer's family business and to BOTLHS author Dr Chris French.

I am most grateful to Andrew Kelsey, who maintains a Twickenham built New Orleans car with the Milnhouse Trust on the Isle of Man, for a host of information, photographs and his profile of 8710 MN. Thanks in particular to Paul Edwards, owner of New Orleans SX 13, for all the details given about his father's monumental rebuild of the car in the 1950s and 1960s, completed with his help. The sketch below *(fig 205)*, also used on the title page, was done by friend of the Edward's family.

Fig 205

Huge thanks to Tom Clarke for sharing his extensive research into the life of Johannes van Toll, for securing the use of the van Toll family photographs (amongst others) and for putting me in touch with motoring writers David Burgess-Wise, Jonathan Wood and Craig Horner. My thanks to them for their help too. Particular thanks to David Hales, his seminal article on New Orleans cars in *The Automobile,* his recent email updates and the use of his photographs. Also to motoring researcher Andrew Minney, in particular for his research into the Carden/AV Monocar and his photographs and to Neil Thorp, owner of two Spikins cars for his help with the Spikins section. Roger Nathan for all his help with the Costin-Nathan sports racing car, his photographs and his stories. Similarly, thanks to Anthony and Robin Rees and family at Mercury Motors, for the use of their family archive and for introducing me to John Paul Jaques, grandson of Robert Bamford. Thanks also to Duncan and Graham Rabagliati, Mark Linstone and particularly his father Cyril who worked with Paul Emery on the Emeryson racing cars in Twickenham in the 1950s. Thank you for all your help with the Emeryson Cars section.

Many thanks to Alan Roe and Rosemary McGlashon for their hard work in preparing the book for publication.

Huge thanks also to Graces Guide to British Industrial History for their generous policy of allowing the use of data and photographs. To my sister Mandy, who discovered an amazing archive of our great grandfather's motoring literature from the 1900s, when sorting through some of our father's things that she'd kept after his death. Finally, to Julia, my wife, for her support and understanding over the last five years … thank you.

Thanks again to all of you.

BOROUGH OF TWICKENHAM LOCAL HISTORY SOCIETY

The Society was formed in 1962 to promote interest in, and record the history of, Twickenham, Teddington, Whitton and the Hamptons. We meet for illustrated talks on the first Monday of the month from October to May in St Mary's Church Hall, Church Street, Twickenham, TW1 3NJ at 8pm. Our newsletter is published three times a year with numerous articles of local historical interest and we have visits to places of interest locally and further afield. The Society is a prolific publisher of historical research papers with over 110 titles, many of which are still in print.

Recent titles include:

- **The Camp on Hounslow Heath**
  (Paper 107) by Ed Harris £9.00
- **Images of Hampton in the 1970s & 1980s**
  (Paper 106) by John Sheaf £7.50
- **"The Regeneration of a Local Community": Fulwell, 1939-2020**
  (Paper 105) by Dr Christopher French £6.50
- **Pictures of Hampton in the 1940s, 1950s & 1960s**
  (Paper 104) by John Sheaf £7.50
- **Kneller Hall: Looking Backward Looking Forward**
  (Paper 103) by Ed Harris £6.00
- **"The Hidden Area of Teddington": The Growth of Fulwell 1870-1939**
  (Paper 102) by Dr Christopher French £6.00
- **Radnor House, Twickenham: The Story of a Thames-side House**
  (Paper 101) by Mike Cherry £5.00
- **"The Italian Murder" and the Slums of Victorian and Edwardian Kingston**
  (Occasional Paper 10) by Dr Christopher French £4.00
- **Images of Hampton in the 1920s and 1930s**
  (Paper 100) by John Sheaf £7.50
- **"A Life Well Led": Richard Gardner (1842-1918) and the City and Metropolitan Police Orphanage, Twickenham**
  (Paper 99) by Dr Christopher French £6.00

For details of all our publications please visit our website at **www.botlhs.co.uk**.
For the latest BOTLHS news, visit our Facebook page: **www.facebook.com/BOTLHS**

Membership information is available from:
Borough of Twickenham Local History Society
Membership Secretary, 87 Fifth Cross Road, Twickenham, TW2 5LJ